MW00559867

HOW TO RAISE A
HEALTHY
GAMER

HOW TO RAISE A
HEALTHY GAMER

End Power Struggles, Break Bad Screen Habits,
and Transform Your Relationship with Your Kids

Alok Kanojia, MD, MPH

RODALE

NEW YORK

Copyright © 2024 by Alok Kanojia

All rights reserved.
Published in the United States by Rodale Books, an imprint of Random House, a
division of Penguin Random House LLC, New York.
rodalebooks.com

Rodale Books is a registered trademark, and the Circle colophon is a trademark
of Penguin Random House LLC.

Library of Congress Cataloging-in-Publication Data

Names: Kanojia, Alok, author.
Title: How to raise a healthy gamer : end power struggles, break bad screen
   habits, and transform your relationship with your kids / by Alok Kanojia.
Identifiers: LCCN 2023031787 | ISBN 9780593582046 (hardcover) |
   ISBN 9780593582053 (ebook)
Subjects: LCSH: Video games and children. | Video gamers—Psychology. |
   Video game—Psychological aspects. | Child rearing.
Classification: LCC HQ784.V53 K36 2023 |
   DDC 794.801/9083—dc23/eng/20230811
LC record available at https://lccn.loc.gov/2023031787

ISBN 978-0-593-58204-6
Ebook ISBN 978-0-593-58205-3

Printed in the United States of America

Book design by Andrea Lau
Jacket design by thebookdesigners
Jacket art by Shutterstock/Nizwa Design
Author photograph by John Winters

10 9 8 7 6 5 4 3 2 1

First Edition

To Kruti, my beloved wife,
who has made this book,
my career, and my life possible

CONTENTS

PART THREE
ACT: Acting on What You Now Know

PART FOUR
COMMON CHALLENGES

HOW TO RAISE A
HEALTHY GAMER

INTRODUCTION

You know your child, right? You've had them in your life for quite some time. You raised that kid—you kissed their bruised knees, you tucked them into bed every night, you made them eat their broccoli. Over time, you helped them with their multiplication tables, maybe taught them your trademark hook shot and how to clear the breakfast dishes. You've loved them through thick and thin, and you've tried to teach them your values along the way.

But when that same beloved kid starts playing a lot of video games, they seem to morph into someone else. Suddenly they aren't your sweet, bright, obedient, funny, mischievous kid anymore. They've become moody and irritable, and their mood swings feel more like the kind of temper tantrums they stopped throwing at age six. When they've been playing a lot of video games, they can turn into someone almost, dare I say, vicious.

No doubt as the fight to control your child's gaming drive has escalated, so, too, has the tension in your home. Your concern grows the more unrecognizable your kid becomes. Even when the problem is relatively small-scale, far from full-blown addiction, there can be frustration. Because when gaming use intensifies, things that used to be easy—like simply getting them to come down for dinner—get a lot harder. You think you're just doing basic things, which you've done for a long time, like trying to get them to walk the dog, and they're yelling at you like you just grounded them for a month. Your child is furious, you're frustrated, and you don't understand what's going on.

Everything, Everywhere, All at Once

It seems as though video games have cropped up around us like mushrooms, and the associated problems—not just addiction but the shortening of attention spans—have skyrocketed, too. And like any invasive species being introduced into a new environment without any regulation, the new species has spread rapidly.

Unfortunately, we have precious few safeguards in place to protect us against harmful technology. Policy makers, medical providers, and tech companies have, at best, been asleep at the wheel, and, at worst, have knowingly created more and more addictive products, carefully studying the landscape to gain an edge—on us and on society as a whole. These companies are constantly trying to build a bigger, better, more *engaging* product, and our protective institutions just haven't been able to keep pace.

That's because anything we have to offer that might counter the spread—academia, government—operates on slower cycles. Research studies on, say, how technology affects the brain, or how harmful screen addiction could be, take three to five years to complete. Those studies have to pile up in bigger and bigger stacks, then be independently verified before institutions such as the American

Psychological Association (APA) will start to make recommendations.

Once they make recommendations, it can take one to two years at a minimum to implement them. Eventually, those changes enter the curriculum of new trainees, who will then spend anywhere between four and ten years in training. And only then will this knowledge be available to the general public.

Meanwhile, the biggest gaming and tech companies are specifically designed to be as agile and innovative as possible. Fortnite, one of the most popular games among the younger teenage set, with over 400 million registered users, is updated every two weeks. Every two to three months, the game releases an entirely new season, essentially a brand-new world for players to discover. How on earth could we possibly keep up with that?

If you've picked up this book, you are likely feeling this kind of dismay! You have a child you feel is spending too much time playing video games. Or you have a child with whom you argue a lot about the time they spend playing video games. Or you have children who are begging you to let them start playing and you want to get ahead of what you think could be a problem down the line. Whatever brings you here, I can help.

Takes One to Know One

I grew up playing video games, just as your kids are. I actually played *a lot* of video games, starting in middle school, all the way through high school. By the time I went off to college, my habit had escalated to an alarming extent. As my parents will attest, I nearly flunked out of college for playing too often.

Unfortunately, I'm not exaggerating. My first year of college, I managed to creep by with less than a 2.0 GPA. My second year wasn't a whole lot better. That was the year I stayed up so late playing video games one night, I slept through my Spanish final. I didn't even try to explain to my professor what happened—I just kind of ghosted him and the whole mortifying situation. My gaming was clearly a problem.

My parents tried everything—restrictions and punishment, freedom and support. Unconditional love. But nothing was working. After two years of college, I flunked out. At that point, we were almost out of options. My parents decided that I needed to get away from my American way of life and move to India, where they had both been born and raised. Even I agreed. It felt drastic, but, at that point, drastic was all I had left. I boarded a plane and moved into an ashram.

That was a revolutionary change for me. In the ashram, I learned that the thoughts in my mind could be controlled. For years I had been struggling to overcome my thoughts, my desires. My mind was constantly thinking about gaming—I was reading about it, talking about it, thinking of trying a new strategy when I went to bed. I was getting distracted when I was walking to class; I was watching videos while I was eating. The idea that I could control my thoughts, rather than my thoughts about gaming being in constant control of me? That changed everything.

I was so taken by these revelations that I decided I wanted to join the group and become a monk, but my teachers there rebuffed me. Becoming a monk was about renouncing your life, they explained. But I had earned nothing thus far, and therefore I had nothing yet to renounce. You're just escaping, they told me. Go become successful first, they said, and come back when you're ready to renounce that success.

So, I headed back to school. In the end, I ended up graduating with about a 2.5 GPA. Something about that number being written in stone—I am a below-average student, and for the rest of my life, I will never be able to change that—threw gasoline on the inner fire that my time in India had ignited. Within eight years of flunking out of college, I would start teaching at Harvard Medical School.

Controlling Your Mind

You don't need to send your child to an ashram in India to "cure" their gaming addiction. But it might help for you to understand why the mindset shift I underwent there changed me so profoundly. According to yogic shastras (ancient texts), the thoughts in our mind can come from two places: our sensory organs and the memory of our sensory organs.

Think about, say, basketball season. If you're surrounded by people talking about last night's game, or you're watching a sports network or listening to sports radio, all these inputs on the subject will populate your mind with thoughts. As your mind gets populated with these thoughts, you will likely engage in talk about basketball even more.

We see this working in both positive and negative ways. For example, a child who is constantly exposed to a certain language will use the same language; they are learning. But the same thing is at work in, for example, children who have experienced trauma. When a child is told day after day that they are worthless, they start to internalize those thoughts. That's also learning, but it certainly isn't healthy or productive.

The challenge you now face is that the game developers are *colonizing your child's mind* with the games themselves, conversations and discussion forums about them, Twitch streams, YouTube shorts, and endless TikToks of gameplay. It's no surprise that your child is constantly thinking of gaming. They simply don't have the power to resist.

Pay attention to the games your child plays. Look at the sounds, the sights, and the colors projected when things happen. For every level they conquer, they get a bright trophy and a satisfying sound. It's so gratifying, sensorily. And so the game sinks even further into your child's mind. This is what you're fighting against—a tide of thoughts in your child's mind. But what you need to do is stop fighting—instead, you need to *decolonize* their mind.

That's why I advocate for small progress—at whatever cost. It's not just the gaming you have to restrict; the more you can shut down or slow down the massive amounts of sensory input they get from gaming—Twitch, YouTube, whatever, it's all the same—the more progress you can make. The less sensory input your child receives, the more they will rediscover their healthy selves.

That's why my Healthy Gamer program works so well: By building an alliance and working a little bit at a time, the *mental colonization of your child's mind will diminish*. As the mental colonization diminishes, they will actually be more willing to speak to you, and they will be more willing to live in a healthy way.

I've worked with thousands of gamers who describe waking up from the "fog" of their gaming years. They say they didn't feel mentally alert during those years, and I certainly know what they mean. I felt the same way. It wasn't until I learned how to control my thoughts, to fill my brain with things other than gaming, that I managed to wake up.

But wake up, I did. After my college graduation, I decided I wanted to become a psychiatrist—equal parts shock and relief for my striving, immigrant parents. Though I had to apply to medical school three times before gaining entry (my undergraduate grades had done me no favors!), I ended up in Boston, training and working at Massachusetts General Hospital and McLean Hospital, both of which are Harvard Medical School teaching affiliates, where I also served as a faculty member.

In med school and in residency, I had the amazing opportunity to learn from some brilliant teachers, people who taught me a lot about psychiatry, yes, but also just about human beings; they helped me figure out how I might be able to spend my life helping people. Not surprisingly, given my track record of struggling with gaming, I was deeply interested in how to help people who have problems with video games.

One of the things I discovered in psychiatry residency, however, was that none of the brightest minds in psychiatry—renowned experts in the field—were able to help me with the gaming issues I had struggled with for so long. For the most part, addiction specialists and child psychiatrists and depression experts and cognitive behavioral experts had no data or experience with these issues. And the more people I asked, the clearer the reason for this became. The most gifted, exceptional minds—the rightfully revered leaders—in the field of psychiatry are all in their fifties, sixties, and seventies. Guess what that means? The majority of them have never even played a modern video game. The glitchy Gameboy of our youth didn't change itself daily to lure us further in. Pong was fun, but there was only so long you could watch that bouncing ball!

It stands to reason that if you've never played a modern video game, you just don't know what the experience is like. And why gaming is so damn addictive. And why it's so hard to convince yourself to turn it off, even when you know it's causing problems in your real life.

So instead of trying to learn more about this pervasive problem from my teachers, I started talking to gamers themselves. Using the emerging technology to meet the gamers in their natural habitat—in Reddit chat rooms, streaming on Twitch, even gaming alongside them, chatting over headphones while we played—I was able to talk to gamers in situ, if you will. I talked to kids from all around the world, from the Middle East and South Korea, rural Canada and urban America, and lots of places in between. I wanted to try to understand them better, so I asked them all kinds of questions about their experiences and, fundamentally, why they played video games in the first place. I heard from a lot of young people who were having the same kinds of problems I'd once struggled with—trouble with their schoolwork and their sleep, tension with their parents, problems figuring out how to just put their controllers down. But the problems seemed even more troubling now—the technology was and is evolving so quickly that a lot of them are in deeper than I was in the early 2000s.

Many of the gamers I spoke to told me that, at their parents' urging, they had finally relented and gone to see a psychiatrist or therapist. Often, they had received a diagnosis—maybe a mood or anxiety disorder—and been started on medication. *Then they went home, took their pills, and just kept playing their video games.* For the most part, I understood why. They might indeed have been depressed or suffering from anxiety—but left untreated was the fact that they played too many video games. They were addicts.

I had been just like them, staying up all night, sleeping through my exams, procrastinating until the last possible minute on every single assignment. *This I understood!* This I could help fix. I'd found my purpose.

In 2018, I posted a message on Reddit explaining that I was a psychiatrist interested in video game addiction. If you have any questions, I said, contact me. The post hit the front page of Reddit, and thousands of questions and comments started pouring in. That's when I realized a lot of people needed help.

Next, I started an online chat server to discuss issues of gaming addiction, and tons of people showed up. I started to get thousands of calls from people who wanted to come see me in my private practice, but I had no capacity to handle the influx of requests. I got some help organizing my efforts, and soon thereafter started Healthy Gamer. I built a coaching curriculum and trained a few coaches, added moderators, hired some people to help turn my Twitch streams into a YouTube channel—and we took off.

These days, with a team of gifted coaches, I help people and organizations with emerging mental health challenges in this increasingly digital world. In creating accessible, inclusive, and affordable mental health resources, Healthy Gamer aims to empower the internet generation to achieve balance and happiness in their lives.

How to Use This Book

My Healthy Gamer program is designed to help foster independence. I encourage restraint, not restriction. Over the past few years, we at Healthy Gamer have helped millions of gamers develop restraint themselves. The strategies I offer in this book have taught countless parents how to help their children develop confidence and independence. Not only does my program help parents teach their gamers how to practice restraint, it also helps parents encourage their children not to develop an unhealthy relationship with gaming in the first place.

When video games are used for enjoyment, not escape, that makes a healthy gamer. Using games to encourage social connection, not enable isolation—that makes a healthy gamer. Using video games to replace social support, or to shore up faltering self-confidence—that leads to *unhealthy* gamers.

Here, in book form, my aim is to take my firsthand knowledge of being a gamer, my years of helping gamers (and their families and partners) at Healthy Gamer, and my training as a psychiatrist, and use it all to help you and your child build a healthy, balanced life. Most important, I am also a parent of two lovely girls who *love* video games. Much of this book comes out of my experiences of raising two children in a technologically invasive world.

My approach is to equip you with a new set of fundamentals for parenting in this technological age. While—as you'll learn below—I do have a suggested timeline for working through the components of my plan, every family is unique, so you should not expect to be "done" after a set period of time. Instead, you should work through the components at your own pace and understand that the conversations you'll be having with your child are never "one and done." I aim to help you change the dynamic with your child, and that's a lifelong change.

My program for raising a healthy gamer has three components, the first of which is to *educate* you, the front line of defense against video game addiction, and the person who loves a gamer enough to read this book. I can appreciate that you probably *just want to get started* with changing your child's behavior, but before you can do that, you need to understand why they are behaving the way they are. That's what part one is all about—three chapters dedicated to helping you understand how games affect your child's neurochemistry and psychology, as well as advice on getting your own mindset ready to take on the issues at hand.

Part two focuses on *talking* to your child about the steps you hope to take together. The chapters in this section include one to help you assess your child's readiness for change, as well as outlining the steps toward that all-important goal of building an alliance with your child. Building an alliance with your child is the most critical dynamic in this program, one that you will lean on heavily as you work through the tough patches in this process. To get there, we'll be working on your *communication skills* to help you connect with and ally with your child, rather than going into battle against them. Once you and your child are on the same team, I will help *you* craft a plan to help *them*, including strategies for dealing with their resistance to it.

Part three is when and where you'll start to *act*. The chapters here cover the process of defining and setting healthy boundaries around gaming and using positive behavioral strategies to enforce them.

From that point onward, you and your child will work *together* to help set and keep them on a healthier, happier path.

Because gaming addiction or problematic gaming behavior often coexists with neurodivergent or mental health issues, part four covers those bases—with information about the "comorbidity" of gaming with ADHD (attention deficit hyperactivity disorder), autism spectrum disorders, depression, anxiety, and marijuana use, as well as suggestions for mitigating these issues with your gamer.

How Long Will This Take?

For most families I work with, this program *works*, but it does not amount to a quick fix. You'll see throughout that I offer you a loose outline of when to introduce what with your child and, if you do the math, you'll work out that it takes two to three months from the initial attempts you make to build an alliance to crafting a plan for implementing boundaries. I've recapped that week-by-week advice in appendix B on page 269, but a lot of this will continue to be fluid.

Sometimes parents and children will need more time to work on trust building or will have to take more time when the child retreats into resistance and stops being a part of the process. Sometimes you will need to problem-solve around boundaries you've set, because things don't always go as planned! Even more commonly, I find that parents themselves can get busy and undergo their own challenges, slowing down the process. On average, I find that the process of continual improvement, with small wins along the way, will help children "recover" from their gaming problem in six to twelve months.

All that said, I urge you to have patience and to take a long view. One of the things I learned during my time in India is that change is not created; it's cultivated. Here in the West, we are all about creating things—we level mountains and build buildings. We are obsessed with outcomes—key performance indicators, closing stock prices, and thirty-day guarantees.

But in the Eastern mindset, it is all about cultivation. My own personal journey has been filled with failure, but that is part of the cultivation of who I am. Think about parenting as the cultivation of your child—you set them up in the right environment, one that will support their growth in the right direction, then you sit back and watch them flourish.

If you want your child to be independent, you can't do all the work for them. You have to let them do the growing; much like the plants in your garden, growth is incremental, and sometimes they are going to want to grow in a slightly different direction.

“

I find that the process of continual improvement, with small wins along the way, will help children “recover” from their gaming problem in six to twelve months.

I know you are intimidated right now. This is a scary time for parents. But I can reassure you that no matter where you are in this challenging, wrenching, emotionally raw journey, *you can do it*. I promise you that every young person out there can be helped. I have seen thousands of gamers recover from unhealthy gaming behavior. Young adults, too. Most of them just need a little help. That's what I'm here for. That's what you're there for. Together, we can do this.

PART ONE

Understand

Understanding Games
and Your Gamer

This section explores the basic reward mechanisms behind video games—and why they appeal to children—in order to equip you with an understanding of why these games are addictive. We'll discuss some neuroscientific concepts regarding addiction, reward, and behavioral reinforcement. Neuroscience begets psychology, so once we understand the basic neuroscientific circuits, we'll see how the brain informs the mind. We'll discuss the basic psychological needs that video games fill: achievement, challenge, identity, community, and safety.

After you understand the basic needs that video games are fulfilling for your child, we can start to create healthier alternatives. Once your child's needs are satisfied through other means, their obsession with playing the game melts away.

CHAPTER I

What Makes Video Games So Addictive?

The Neurochemistry of Gaming Explained

When I am working with parents—parents like you, who have grown increasingly concerned with the direction their kids are headed—the first question most of them ask me is this: *Is my kid addicted to video games*? I mean, they know their child has a problem. Most of them have noticed some changes in their kids' behavior, ones that worry them. Maybe their grades are slipping. They're more isolated than they used to be. They're a little bit more moody. But, *Dr. K, is this actually an addiction?* they ask.

There's a lot of debate on the topic. In 2018, the World Health Organization (WHO) identified something called "internet gaming disorder." But there's another group of people who don't think that gaming is an addiction in the same way as alcohol or opiates can be. And these two camps argue endlessly about which one of them is right. But, frankly, to me? It really doesn't matter whether a group of psychiatrists agree on the terms of an addiction diagnosis. The so-called experts can battle that one out on the internet or in dueling research papers. This is about you and your kid.

> ❝
>
> Whether a group of psychiatrists agree on the terms of an addiction diagnosis doesn't matter. The so-called experts can battle that one out on the internet or in dueling research papers. This is about you and your kid.

If their gaming is causing a problem within your household, if it's causing a problem for their future, then chances are it's a problem, right? Whether we label it an addiction or not isn't actually the point. The real point is that they need to move forward, to a better, healthier relationship with technology, whether they cross the threshold of "addiction" or not.

And, of course, sometimes it's not just children and teenagers we're worrying about. Some people who walk through our virtual door at Healthy Gamer are concerned about their adult child, perhaps the twenty-three-year-old who's living in their basement. Is that person not moving in the direction that they need to be moving in? Are they having problems at school or problems at work? Are they even going to school or work? Are they getting moody, or throwing temper tantrums, or just being generally disrespectful?

From an academic standpoint, the common factor for all mental illness—addictions included—is that it interferes with your life. No matter the substance, *addiction* means "an impairment of function." And many of the kids and young adults I've met in the past several years certainly have an impairment of function.

Bottom line: If you think it's a problem, it is a problem. You don't need an expert to tell you that. You are their parent. That makes you the expert.

Neuroscience Helps Explain Why Your Child Is Changing

In order to help your child, it's really important for you to understand a few things about *why* they are playing video games. I want to help you appreciate the vital underlying needs that are being met when they play video games. These needs are firmly embedded in the teenage brain, as old as time, and, for what it's worth, totally normal. To start, it's important to understand the circuits in the brain that play a part in why your child loves gaming so much.

Reward Circuitry

When you read about or hear talk of addictions, the first term you're likely to hear tossed around is *dopamine*. Dopamine is what scientists call a "neurotransmitter," which is a chemical signal one neuron uses to talk to another—basically, ways for our brain to communicate.

Dopamine happens to be one of the major neurotransmitters—but its effect depends on which neurons are involved. In the substantia nigra, a very small structure in our mid-brain, dopamine is used to help us move our muscles in a smooth and coordinated fashion. In Parkinson's disease, for example, the dopamine-production neurons in the substantia nigra get destroyed, which is why people with Parkinson's have difficulty with movement. This is why we give Parkinson's patients dopamine as medicine.

But dopamine is mostly known for its involvement in reward and behavioral reinforcement because it is the primary neurotransmitter of our reward circuitry, a cluster of nerves located in the Nucleus Accumbens (NAcc) of the brain. Achievement, success, triumph, pleasure—these are all mediated by dopamine being released in the NAcc.

Dopamine is also involved in *shaping behavior*, because whenever we get that dopamine release in the NAcc, we "feel good"—and when we "feel good," we repeat the behaviors.

A good example of this: Historically, calorie-dense foods have led to survival. When something increases our chances of survival, we have evolved to enjoy it. As a result, what we think of as "pleasure" is just our brain pointing us in a direction and saying, "Do more of this, because this is good for us." Since this thing is good for us, we are going to crave it again. Then when we eat that thing again, we get a *second release of dopamine*, which makes us feel pleasure and reinforces the behavior. If eating a calorie-rich food leads to pleasure, or enjoyment, we tend to look for it again—this is anticipation. Dopamine governs all three of these responses—pleasure, reinforcement, and anticipation—all of which evolved to help us survive.

The problem is, in today's world, one signal that governs all three things can get hijacked by video games. Game designers have figured out how to control our dopamine switch, offering us all that pleasure, reinforcement, and anticipation, but without contributing a survival benefit.

Dopamine isn't the enemy here, not at all. Even in our modern world, dopamine can help us learn and grow. A helpful analogy is the process of learning to play a piece of music. The first time you sit down to try to play it, you may struggle a little. You make a mistake, you make another mistake, but, eventually, if you keep at it, you'll learn how to play the piece properly. The satisfaction that you get when you succeed after failure is also mediated by dopamine. The harder something is, the more we feel challenged, the more dopamine gets released *when we succeed*. When something is challenging, and we fail at it a few times before we succeed, that success feels especially good, and that kind of success-seeking behavior gets reinforced.

Game designers have gotten especially good at figuring out how to maximize that dopamine release in the brain. They know that if the game is too easy, people get bored and leave. If the game is too challenging, they'll quit, because the dopamine release isn't worth the effort. So, game designers titrate the difficulty to optimize dopamine release—thus reinforcing the behavior, and maximally increasing anticipation.

Recent research shows this—that the reason video games are addictive is not necessarily just because they provide a reward, but because they actually deny you the reward for an extended period of time. Like learning that piece of music—we actually want to play and fail over and over, because when we finally succeed, it feels really good.

The tricky thing, though, is that our brain has a natural tendency to achieve homeostasis, or balance; for this reason, our brain can start to develop tolerance for particular things. The first cookie you eat is very tasty; the second one is pretty good, too. But after you've polished off three or four more cookies, you probably can barely even taste them, let alone enjoy them.

That's exactly what we see with video games—eventually, with hours of play, the dopamine circuits can develop physiological tolerance. *Tolerance* is the principle of our brain balancing things to keep them within a "normal" or healthy range. If anything rises above that range, we'll modulate the high external signal by adjusting the volume and turning down the signal. Think of it like a music player and a set of headphones: If the volume is too high to listen to comfortably, we can turn down the volume to keep the experience enjoyable.

What happens with video games is that our dopamine signals get jacked up, then our *dopamine receptors* downregulate—literally turning down the "volume" on the dopamine signal. We essentially are removing receptors from our neurons, so that even a *ton of dopamine release* leads to a "regular" amount of enjoyment.

Now the problem is that if we stop playing video games and read a book, we'll get a "normal" amount of dopamine signal, but with our downregulated receptors, the total "volume" is too low—thus making reading feel not at all fun. Our brain is physically less capable of enjoying reading when we game too much.

You may have observed this in your child even when it comes to gaming itself. For the first hour or so that they're playing video games, they're having fun. But by the time they've been playing for four hours, they're not having fun anymore—they're just zombies who've stopped smiling and laughing and talking. Furthermore, anytime you try to get them to do anything besides the video game, they just feel bored all the time, and they resist it with all their strength, right? That's because of the dopamine tolerance—if they've been playing endless hours of video games, it is going to take some time for them to get acclimated to enjoying other activities.

The Amygdala

Well, if it isn't even fun, why do kids keep going back to it, over and over again? Why do they keep playing? Games are addictive not just because they feel good, but also because they diminish bad feelings. All addictive substances share two properties—they not only give pleasure, but they also take away pain.

Cue our discussion of the amygdala. The amygdala is a big player in our limbic system, the part of the brain that produces emotions. The amygdala is in charge of what we might call our "survival emotions," the ones that are active when we are in danger, like fear or anxiety. These emotions are vital for our ability to predict and respond to danger.

Our survival emotions used to be activated for short bursts in the wild—say, if we saw a tiger or a snake. But in today's world, they tend to be chronically elevated—for adults, we feel stress when it comes to paying our mortgage, or seeking a promotion, or our plans to retire. In kids, they get activated by academic stress, bullying, and social media.

In the past, when the danger went away—i.e., we ran away from the snake or the tiger—the fear shut off. But nowadays, the problems we face are more chronic—even if you pay your mortgage this month, you still have to pay it next month. Kids, for their part, have to worry about tests and bullying pretty much every day.

Neuroscientific evidence shows that video games suppress the emotional circuitry. Essentially, gaming suppresses or shuts off the amygdala, providing us with temporary relief from daily stress. To be fair, this is true of just about any form of recreation. If you've had a hard day at work, going to a bar to have a couple of drinks or watching some TV to unwind also helps suppress the negative emotions stemming from your stressful day.

But any activity that successfully suppresses our negative emotions also has the tendency to be addictive. After all, if we're feeling bad, or stressed out, or ashamed, or afraid, and we can engage in some kind of behavior that temporarily makes those feelings go away, that behavior can be very reinforcing. All of those problems simply fade into the background, and we're just focused on the one thing that feels good.

This is exactly what's going on with video games—functional MRI (fMRI) studies (which spotlight levels of brain activity) have shown that if we're experiencing fear, anger, frustration, sadness, or any other negative emotion, and we then start to play video games, our amygdala begins to calm down. Our emotions get suppressed. That is why gaming is such an "effective" coping mechanism.

I remember this very well from back when I was at my worst in college. I knew that every day that I skipped Spanish class contributed to me falling further behind. I knew that even if I went to class, my grades would still be awful, and my Spanish was getting worse. I couldn't fix the problem, and I knew it, and I felt awful about it. The only solution? Make the pain go away through gaming.

I used to go to sleep at 4 or 5 a.m., because if I went to bed earlier, all the worry and fear I carried with me—that I was ruining my life—would flood into my mind and I wouldn't be able to sleep. I would game to the point of absolute exhaustion, so that the second my head hit the pillow, I would just pass out. That's how badly I wanted to keep the negative thoughts at bay. Then I'd wake up after having slept through class once again. Class was over? Oh, well. I'd boot up the game, start playing, and the cycle would begin anew. Run from bad feelings, game more, fall further behind, repeat.

Your child might know that they are screwing up their life—or at least starting to head down that path. But they know that if they turn off the video games, they'll have too much time to think about the science test they just failed, or how disappointed you guys are going to be that they lied and skipped karate class all week long. They keep playing so they don't have to think about all that negative stuff.

To make matters worse, once your child has started outsourcing the regulation of their emotions to video games, their capacity to deal with negative emotions without gaming shrinks. And as their coping capacity shrinks, the emotions they've been burying in gaming in the first place start to leak out in other ways. This is why your kids may be throwing temper tantrums or getting frustrated too easily. You may also see other strange, but related, behaviors that you don't realize are tied to emotions—like isolation, withdrawal, sarcasm, or cynicism.

Bottom line: When your child seems really addicted to gaming, the issue is not simply a dopamine rush anymore. It's a dependency on the emotional regulation that video games provide. The more the gaming behavior suppresses the amygdala, the more of an escape gaming will be for your child.

The Frontal Lobes

This leads us to the third circuit of the brain that's important to understand: the frontal lobes, which basically govern maturity. A fifteen-year-old is more mature than a five-year-old, and a twenty-five-year-old is even more mature. But what does this capacity for maturity actually mean? A five-year-old can't regulate their emotions; they can't plan ahead, nor can they delay gratification very well. Teenagers can be a little bit more responsible; they can handle some amount of delayed gratification, and they can usually focus on what they need to focus on. A twenty-five-year-old has a pretty high level of impulse control and ability to delay gratification—for the most part, they can wake up every day and get themselves to work.

That's our frontal lobes at work, helping out with impulse control and emotional regulation; our frontal lobes control the amygdala and the limbic system. They don't always work perfectly, of course—as each of us knows all too well. There are times when you feel stressed out and get frustrated with your kid. Sometimes that frustration gets the better of you, and you lose your temper and yell. But other times, you manage to rein in that frustration and exercise a little bit more control. When that happens, that's your frontal lobes activating.

The problem with video games is that they're so engaging, we don't need to force our mind to focus. No one gets distracted playing video games—game designers take care of the focusing part for you. As a result, your focusing capability in your frontal lobes atrophies. Gamers lose the ability to control their mind, to force it to focus. Then, when they try to do something in the real world, they can't focus. Studying feels nearly impossible, because their brain has gotten so dependent on highly engaging entertainment to keep it focused on one thing.

If your child plays a lot of video games, they have started to rely on the games to regulate their emotions, which means they have stopped strengthening their frontal lobes. Gaming is essentially the opposite of meditation in terms of the effect it has on your frontal lobes. People who game too much essentially put the development of their maturity on hold. Brain scan studies bear this out. Gamers tend to have underdeveloped frontal lobes compared to non-gamers. Fact: From a neuroscientific perspective, gamers are actually more immature than non-gamers.

The Hippocampus

The last brain architecture concept that we need to understand as parents of gamers is the hippocampus. Very closely connected to the amygdala and our other emotional circuits, the hippocampus is worth calling separate attention to because it is believed to be the place where memories are made and stored and, therefore, is the center of learning. As video games suppress the amygdala, they also suppress the amygdala's ability to access the hippocampus. As a result, gamers have a hard time *learning* from their mistakes.

Usually, if we do something and are hurt by it, we don't do it again, because negative emotions are powerful influencers of behavior. Think of it this way: You eat at a restaurant five times, and you love it—you're a big fan. Then you go a sixth time and get a miserable case of food poisoning. Even though you really liked the restaurant before, that one bad plate of food will make you very reluctant to go back. I see this same aversion to what's learned through negative emotions when I work with patients who have struggled with infidelity. You can be married to someone for fifteen years, and all it takes is one act of infidelity, that strong sense of betrayal, and the way you interact with your spouse might change forever. This one event might even change how you interact with future partners.

Negative emotional experiences trigger our brain to learn—mistakes are the greatest teacher. But gamers short-circuit this pathway by suppressing their negative emotions through video games. Once we disable our negative emotions, our learning circuitry becomes inactive. Gamers aren't learning from their mistakes, because whatever that failure was—small or large—they aren't feeling the pain of it. They might fail a test or procrastinate up to the very last minute, and they can swear to you that they want to change, but the next day, there are no changes in their behavior. And it isn't that they don't understand or feel regret, *in the moment*. They aren't lying. Despite having a lengthy talk in which you both seemed to agree, the conversation doesn't seem to have been saved to the hard drive. They don't incorporate what they've learned into long-term memory. In one ear and out the other.

Even though your child actually does understand the changes they need to make, that part of their brain—the one that rewrites the code—has been shut off by video games. Basically, their amygdala's ability to access the hippocampus and teach them something gets compromised.

The not-so-virtuous cycle continues. Video games suppress the circuitry governing negative emotions and disrupt the learning circuitry, but playing games also causes the brain to release dopamine, remember? And that makes your child feel better. When a child fails a test because they were playing too many video games, but the dopamine-addled part of their brain tells them it was fun to do so, they're going to wake up the next day to play games again and never learn their lesson.

This is why it seems so confusing for you. Despite all your best efforts, your child just doesn't seem to be getting it. It's not sinking in. In the past, they've learned from their mistakes, but, now, their brain circuits are being disrupted by technology—their development has been hijacked by the game developers.

And these game developers aren't stopping with just their neurochemistry—they know your kids have psychological needs, and they've figured out ways to hijack those, too.

CHAPTER 2

Why Are Our Kids
So Obsessed?

How Gaming Meets Psychological Needs

Although the teenage brain hasn't changed much over the course of human history, the world around it certainly has. Technology is the biggest game changer and that, in turn, has made our kids' socialization very different than it was even a short time ago. And that's not all. Technology has also changed how they have fun and how they develop identities.

Consider this: Twenty years ago, if you were getting bullied in school, your options were to try to defend yourself using harsh words or physical violence or to ask for help from a parent or teacher or school administrator. Or you'd hide your shame and probably tell no one, and just learn to deal with it. Whichever way you chose to deal with the humiliation you felt, you were still the same awkward, uncomfortable you when you went to school the next day. There was no escaping *you*.

Gaming gives kids a way to escape and a new way to change their reputation. It offers a world in which they don't experience any judgment, where they don't feel humiliated or shamed or pitied. Gaming provides a safe haven—an imaginary place where children have real peers, even teammates, who witness them crushing opponents and who celebrate their gaming accomplishments in a place where they can *control* their world.

"

Gaming provides a safe haven—an imaginary place where children have real peers, even teammates, who witness them crushing opponents and who celebrate their gaming accomplishments in a place where they can *control* their world.

I'll give you an example. Let's say everyone is playing soccer on the playground at recess. But you suck at soccer. Imagine if your teacher then tells you that you don't have to play and instead suggests you go sit in the library. That teacher has just offered you a judgment-free zone—it's different, it's safe, and for the kids who can't handle soccer, it's fantastic.

You might be thinking that I'm going to say that the virtual world is like the library in this analogy, but it's more than that. The virtual world is way better than the library. Not only is it a place where you don't get judged (or don't have to listen to the judging), it's a place where you *control the rules of soccer*. So, you're not even being sidelined—you're still playing, but the game is rigged in your favor. And that's what makes it so addictive. (It's just like on social media—take Instagram or TikTok filters. It isn't that people don't judge you on your appearance, it is that you can rig the game to your benefit.)

We all want to feel safe, to feel part of a community, to feel like we can be ourselves. Video games allow kids to be who they wish they were, to assume an identity of their own choosing, one that hasn't been assigned to them at birth. Online, they're who they see themselves as—someone without acne or glasses; someone who's not overweight or too skinny or frail; someone who has enough money or, if having too much has made them uncomfortable, is no longer ogled for what they *do* have; someone who is a fast runner or an excellent athlete. Of course, being that "better" version of themselves is going to be addictive.

When you take that computer away from your child, you are thrusting them right back into the world of bullying and judgment. You're actually taking away the one place where they feel secure and confident in who they are. Because when you take that safe, comfortable world away from your kid, you're damning them to a life of math worksheets and Snapchat stories that are telling them everyone else is having more fun than they are. You're making them live in a world where they are average rather than exceptional, where they may feel like less of a person than the other people in their class. Who wants to be a B student in real life if they can be number one on the leaderboard in their online universe?

Your Child's Core Needs

All humans have the same basic physical needs: food, water, air, and shelter. Psychologically, we all have needs, too. Specifically, those needs are for challenge and achievement, identity and a safe space in which to assert it, and community. Kids feel the need for these things most acutely, so let's look at each of them in turn and through the lens of how video games meet them.

Challenge and Achievement

Why do human beings relish success?

The answer lies in evolutionary biology. The ageless human narrative—from our hunter-gatherer forebears to Odysseus to Frodo Baggins—is that of us heading out into the unknown, overcoming an obstacle, and returning with a reward, triumphant. Psychologists coined the term *intent to mastery*, to indicate that a human is driven to exert a massive amount of effort to achieve something difficult and valuable; this is a pattern that is hardwired into our circuitry. The intent to mastery is the core reason that infants don't give up when learning to walk. If you think about it, infants fail over and over again when learning how to walk, or even pick up objects. But there's something hardwired into our brain to keep trying, even when things are difficult. This intent to mastery also manifests at a societal level, where we respect and value people who accomplish difficult things—Olympic athletes, world-class pianists, Fields medalists.

Video game designers have done a great job of tapping into this drive. There are challenges and rewards at every level. When a gamer beats an opponent or jumps to the next level of play, they get this much-craved sense of accomplishment and a little rush of "Yeahhhh!" Game designers understand this all too well and strive to strike the balance between making the game challenging enough so you feel like you accomplished something and easy enough not to create frustration. That is the sweet spot where games are the most engaging, and video game developers know it.

You may recall from our discussion of the brain circuitry in chapter 1 that the little rush you get from accomplishing something challenging is attributable to dopamine, the neurotransmitter that gets triggered by achievement after frustration. Related to this is something called the "triumph circuit." The feeling of triumph we get, from a psychological perspective, is more than just dopamine. Our own sense of identity, respect, and pride comes from our triumphs.

But this quirk of human psychology was supposed to help motivate us to achieve difficult things in life. It was not meant to be exploited artificially in the way video games have done. The downside of this is that gamers who are addicted to video games no longer need to solve real-world problems to feel triumphant. As a result, they get stuck—their achievements with the game trigger a feeling of triumph, which effectively robs them of their motivation to move forward in real life.

As we'll discuss later on, I have found that the kids who need my help the most are not the kids who have trouble in school—they're the ones who come from high-achieving families, who often find school too easy. As much as parents—let alone teachers—hate to admit it, a lot of the time, school is just boring. Even in the best of situations or at the most rigorous schools, teachers have to follow a state-mandated curriculum, they have to teach with standardized tests in mind, and they have to slow down substantially for the students who haven't caught on yet.

Games, on the other hand, are designed to be perfectly challenging—you don't win right away, but you do eventually win. Compared to real life, where challenges can result in failure, games offer the perfect level of dopamine, a result of that reward circuitry. Psychologically, we want to feel challenged and "overcome" our challenges. When a child faces real-world failure, which may be difficult or impossible to "overcome," the video game is there for them.

Video games are intellectually dazzling. The game you are playing moves at whatever speed you do, but is still always a step ahead of you. You don't have to slow down for anyone, nor do you have to convince a real-world friend to join you—as much as you want to practice and play, the game is there for you, always ready, always able to keep up, and so are your gaming peers.

The other comforting thing about video games is you'll never be left behind. If you're having trouble with a level, you can keep trying it until you get it right. If only real life offered such reassurance.

You can achieve triumph and success in the real world—but at a risk, and with a high price. You can train hard to win the Olympics and never even make the team. Years of effort, wasted. There are no guarantees in the real world. But in the game? The game is rigged to ensure that you succeed—but also to make it just hard enough to trick your brain into thinking the success is as valuable, and difficult, as real-world success. How can the real world ever compete with that?

Identity and a Safe Place to Assert It

Closely related to the need to be safe is the human need to define our own identity, which is not something any of us is born with—it's something that develops over the full course of childhood.

Babies, for instance, don't have a conception of themselves or anything else. They simply have needs, and they're happy or unhappy in any given moment. They can't tell the difference between being hungry or having a dirty diaper—they're either content, or they're not content. Then, over time, around age two or three, they start to develop a sense of themselves. They have certain preferences, they have likes and dislikes. But they don't quite yet understand that Mommy and Daddy are their own beings, separate from them, a human being who has their own thoughts and feelings and hopes and fears. They just don't know that other people exist. (As an aside, this is why trauma is so devastating to children. Because if you're the only person who exists in the world, if you're the only thinking, feeling object, anything bad that happens to you is your fault because there's no one else out there who's responsible.)

Around the age of nine or ten, kids start to develop an idea that there are other people out there, but those people remain pretty one-dimensional. They sort of recognize that Uncle Joe likes me, and Uncle Bob does not. But it's a step. Then when we hit the teenage years, the period when our body starts to enter the phase of sexual maturation, our brain enters a complementary phase: We start to learn how to find mates. For the first time, we start to understand that other people have nuanced and lasting opinions about us.

37

This is why teenagers are so anxious and lacking in confidence in themselves. They have finally figured out that—uh-oh—what they do or what they say or how they dress will actually change people's opinions about them. Now they don't want to say the wrong thing. They don't want to dress the wrong way. For the most part, they want to fade into the background and avoid all that judgment.

As you become an adult, you start to develop a sense of internal identity—you have a sense of who you are, so if people make fun of you, you can weather the storm because you know who you are. But a teenager doesn't have that internal sense of confidence—their brain just hasn't developed that way yet—so adolescence is an exceptionally vulnerable period.

During this vulnerable time, bullying starts taking a toll; this is why people form cliques, which are a form of protection. It's also why your kid suddenly starts caring a ton about how their hair looks, what they're wearing, and that all the popular kids have the latest cool sneakers, and they are angry that you won't spring for a pair for them. Or they reject the whole system and feel like a misfit—which is still caring, in a backhanded way. Your teenager is hyperaware and alert to all these seemingly inconsequential social things; they might seem unimportant to you, but try to remember what it was like when you were a teenager. I always felt like I was on the cusp of having everything figured out, but I was constantly coming up *just* short. Fitting in—or trying to figure out how to, anyway—is vital to their own sense of security and survival.

Here, again, video games meet their needs, since they give players a chance to determine who they will be. In real life, your kid might struggle with being overweight, or being prone to acne, or just feeling socially awkward. Online, that same child might be at the top of the leaderboard, respected and feared. In other words, the game makes it easy for us to build an identity we can be proud of, whereas real life makes it hard.

Bullying has always existed, but these days it's risen to a whole different level. When you were growing up, bullying happened in the classroom, maybe on the school bus before school, or on the playground during recess, right? When we were kids, even if there was a bully, we could go home and our classmate/tormentor was no longer there.

But today, there are very few safe spaces anymore. A bully can follow you home, because they're on Instagram, they're on Twitter, they're on Snapchat, and they can continue to judge and mock you at all hours of the day.

So some kids find refuge in video games. Because the online world is a *safe space.*

You don't get to choose who you are in the real world, especially not when you're an adolescent. In the real world, it takes months or even years to get physically fit. Online, with the click of a few buttons, you are ripped. Online, you can decide who you want to be, how you want to look, what you want to say—without anyone reminding you who your loser real-life self is. Online, you are free.

The more your child starts to invest in the game, and therefore their online identity, their IRL identity starts to fade into the background. Then it becomes harder to "catch up" in the real world—they're just falling further and further behind in developing a real-life identity they are proud of. So, their logic goes, why not invest more in the virtual world? Your child has probably found that it takes less effort—and involves less heartbreak—to achieve in the virtual world. There is efficiency there—if they lean further into the virtual world, they get to be who they want to be, and faster. But soon enough, they end up getting stuck, and then their virtual identity is all they have.

Community

Video games offer people a sense of community, a way to connect, one that might be particularly lacking elsewhere in their own lives. For kids who have trouble making new friends, or who feel awkward in social settings, or who have recently moved to a new town, an online community is a huge draw. The games kids are playing today have been designed to offer them exactly that.

When I was in grade school, we had a gaming system in our basement that we just turned on and played. No internet—just me and maybe a neighbor, because we only had two controllers. That was the extent of my gaming community. But then gaming evolved to allow a lot of different people to play at once—friends nearby, but also people all over the world.

When I was about fifteen, I got really into a game called Starcraft, and I started playing it a lot with one particular online opponent, a guy whose screen name was Error. After playing together every day for quite a while, I eventually learned that his name was Chris, he was around my age, and he lived in a nearby state.

Over the years, we continued to play with and against each other, and we kept in touch through our gaming. I played with him in high school, then when my high school friends all split up and went away to college, I kept gaming with this guy. I lost touch with a lot of my high school friends, but Chris stayed with me. Ditto after college and into med school—even as my friend groups changed, he was my one constant.

He was one of those friends I always carried with me. I've taken him with me throughout all my life changes—he's "seen" me grow and change and he's grown and changed, too. I met the woman who is now my wife when I was twenty-one years old—and he was at the other end of my video game line throughout the entire time I got to know her.

When it came time to get married, I realized that he was one of my closest friends. But we had never once met in person, until he arrived at my bachelor party. My wife met him at the wedding for the first time, but even though she'd never seen him before, she recognized his voice, because she'd heard him speak to me for over a decade through speakers. She knew him, too.

So even though most of this relationship occurred online, my friendship with Chris is authentic to me—it's real, even if you find it hard to understand that a virtual relationship could feel so real to the people who are in it. Chris has been my friend, a true friend, for longer than most of my actual IRL friends.

This is how your child is likely experiencing community online, too. And some of the people they "meet" online are people who value them for the person they feel they are—not the everyday, physical identity they've gotten stuck with. And those people choose to get online every day and reach out to your son or daughter and ask to hang out! Just pause and think about that for a second. How amazing is that for your child? There is someone out there who is always wanting to hang out. Wouldn't that make you feel good?

If your son gets dumped by his friend group, or your daughter switches schools, or your family moves to a new town, all their friends are going to be gone. We often see a big increase in gaming time and addiction when families move, because moving when you're a kid really sucks. It's hard for most people to jump right in and meet new people, but for the child who has trouble making real-life friends, it's that much harder. But their online community is portable, so after they've gone through a difficult move, that child will likely lean into it and depend on that online group even more. The people from the internet are still going to be there for them.

Soon enough, their real life falls by the wayside because the community they have formed online feels stronger, more solid, and just more real to them than the so-called real world that keeps changing around them. What parents don't understand is that if you try to take away their games, you're also taking away their social connections. You think it's just a game. But it's not. These are your child's people. They are their community. Imagine if someone restricted you from seeing your family and friends for a weekend—you'd resist, wouldn't you? This is what parents run into—that is why their children are so resistant.

If you want them to stop playing video games, you can't just take away their community without giving them back a community of another kind. The solution is to help your child build an alternative community of support. Once they have a real-world community, they'll be more amenable to letting go of their online community. There are some interactions in the real world that we naturally prefer—even gamers crave real-life interaction; they just might need a bit more help finding it.

That's what you're there for—to help. You have to build another community *with* them. And if you do it together, it will help with alliance-building—you'll be on the same side. Together, you will have the opportunity *to build a better community*, where they feel safe, supported, challenged, connected, and, maybe most important, a place where they like themselves. And they will love you for this because you will have demonstrated that you understand them and their needs.

The Dark Side of Anonymity

Although the amazing judgment-free zone of the internet is a wonderful thing for a lot of kids, we all know that there's an equally awful and toxic part of the internet—I call it the "dark side of anonymity." Crime tends not to happen in the sunlight—it happens in the shadows. And the internet is just one gigantic shadow, because no one knows who you are. That causes people to unveil some of the darker, nastier parts of themselves on the internet.

In real life, human beings are kept in check by morals, by laws, by societal norms, or by the consequences of our actions. Our behavior is constrained because we are being held accountable in one way or another. We'd like to think it's mostly because we have a sense of right and wrong, but research has shown that there are two factors that make employees more likely to steal from their employers. Sorry to tell you—it's not morals; it's opportunity and being able to get away with it. I don't walk down the street and steal $100 from someone, maybe because I morally object to stealing, but maybe also because that person would see me, and they'd tell the cops or my parents that I was the one who stole their money. And there are going to be consequences if my identity is known. People robbing a bank wear ski masks for a reason.

We talked earlier about the loss of safe spaces. Remember back when you took your child to the playground? As a parent, you were generally aware of the people interacting with your child. If there had been a crowd of strangers in their thirties or forties who started talking to your child at a playground or after school, how would you have reacted? You'd have intervened pretty damn quickly.

But this is exactly what happens on the internet—you're just not there to see it. There is no geographical or proprietary barrier that keeps people apart. You have no idea who is interacting with your child, and, perhaps even scarier, you have no control over it. Sure, the people they meet online might end up at their wedding someday, but they also might just be groomers, or perverts, or creeps.

If your kid is playing video games, there's a decent chance that they might be hearing things that are too brutal for me to repeat—just really nasty stuff to and about other human beings. Maybe even scarier? There is a chance your child is saying that stuff, too.

The anonymity of the internet allows people to do things that they would never do in person, and it breeds a lot of toxic behavior. A friend of mine recently told me that their ten-year-old son had been playing a lot of Fortnite on his computer. He always wore headphones when he was talking to people he was playing with. One night, my friend put some headphones on and listened in for a little while. He was horrified to realize he was listening to some twenty-six-year-old guy telling his ten-year-old child to go f*ck himself. That's not the kind of language that we let our children watch on TV, but when they play video games, there are people using those words and *directing* those words *at them*. Sometimes the language is sexually explicit. Sometimes it's racist. It's often misogynistic. It's brutal, and there is no PG-rated section your kids can hang out in—the R- (or even X-) rated stuff is everywhere. And it's not just other people's behavior you have to worry about. If your child is playing video games, there's a decent chance that they might be talking in a way that you would find absolutely shocking.

I'm not trying to scare you. And I'm not saying that you should unplug the video game. This will be your instinct—of course it will. Your fears are valid! Your instinct is to shut down the thing that is scaring you, that is threatening your child. You've probably already tried this. But when you give in to that fear, you are met with resistance, with anger, with resentment, with a breakdown of communication between you and your child. And that is not what we want. You are depriving them of their community when you shut down their gaming entirely, and they will always resist that.

Our goal is not to insulate them from the danger that is out there. Your job is to help them navigate shark-infested waters in the hope of leading them toward safety.

Instead of shutting down the thing that you fear, you need to get involved. Our goal at Healthy Gamer is to prepare kids for the world they live in, not to put our heads in the sand. The best medicine against the toxicity of the internet is to get more involved in your child's life and to understand the community that they're a part of. Once you understand it, you can help safely guide them through this world.

Anticipatory Guidance: Setting Limits for Younger Kids

If your child is just starting to play video games online or is young enough for you to still have some control and influence on their behavior, there are several things you can do to get ahead of potential problems.

- Limit or disable the voice-chat capabilities on your household system so that they can't just talk to whoever they want to. Most video games have "sound settings" in which you can choose to disable voice chat. Some games allow you to individually mute players once a game starts. I recommend globally disabling it in the game sound settings for young children.
- Make a rule that they need to use speakers—and not headphones—so you can walk by at any time and hear what's going on. They're much less likely to engage in the darker stuff if others can hear them doing it.
- In addition to being able to hear what's going on, make sure you can see it, too. Environment is key; keep the gaming in a place where you can monitor it. Multiple studies have found that having a game in a child's room increases usage—an increase of up to 50 percent. If you've let your child have a game console in his bedroom—and allow him to play with the bedroom door closed—you are ceding important environmental controls.

CHAPTER 3

Why Are Parents Struggling So Much with This?

How to Adapt to Parenting in a Technological World

I f you are feeling overwhelmed and remarkably lonely on this issue of parenting through gaming dependence, you are not alone! Your friends might not be openly talking about it, but many are struggling with these big issues and big feelings, too.

As I said earlier, part of being overwhelmed comes from the fact that policy makers and institutions move too slowly to keep up with the pace of technology; and we parents and caregivers need them to move faster. There is a reason the problem feels completely out of hand. But, as I also said earlier, the issue is exacerbated by the fact that video games are less a "new territory" to today's parents than they are a whole new planet!

Think about the world your children are growing up in as opposed to the world your own parents raised you in. The gap is almost unfathomably huge. The parenting techniques that we internalized from our own parents don't translate very well to the digital age. Our parents never needed to monitor television use twenty-four hours a day, because cartoons only came on for a few hours on weekend mornings, and there was usually only one screen and one remote control. Parents today have to learn a new set of skills—ones that we've never had to know before.

For example, many of the kids out there gaming right now truly believe they are going to go pro, no matter how middling their skills. This wasn't a battle my parents had to fight, as the professional gaming ecosystem didn't exist when I was a kid. (For the record, we have researched this at Healthy Gamer. Our conclusion: We have found that attempting to become a professional gamer is, on a surface level, an irresponsible financial decision, and that the statistics on success are minimal. Don't argue with your child about this—just ask him to show you statistical proof of what his chances of going pro are.)

Beyond having absurd conversations about future professional gaming salaries, there are yet more lessons for you to learn ahead. You are going to have to learn new ways to share—sometimes for the first time—and even fully hand over responsibility to your child to manage their own behavior. This requires managing your own emotions and guilt, so that you can think clearly as you navigate this incredibly complex, emotionally difficult time as a parent. Honing these new skills first requires owning up to the need for them!

Learning to Cede Responsibility—and Failure

One of the thorniest problems that you are likely to face with a child who has problem behavior with video gaming is dealing with failure—your own and your child's. It's completely natural and reasonable not to want your child to fail; you've long since internalized the idea that you are responsible for protecting your children from failure. You're also probably feeling that any of their failings are, by extension, your own failings, too. No one wants to face these issues!

When I speak in person to parent groups at schools, I always ask the crowd an opening question: Who has the power in your relationship with your child? Of course, most parents initially say the "right" thing—that they hold the power. But then I ask who has the responsibility for getting things done on time? Inevitably, most parents say that is their child's responsibility.

Okay, I ask out loud, when your child doesn't do their homework, who makes sure that they remember? Who reminds them to go to tae kwon do practice? Who wakes them up in time for school? Who does all of that for them? Lots of parents start shuffling their feet when we get to this point. Because, they start to concede, they themselves are actually bearing the responsibility of getting things done, let alone done on time. Our kids are not responsible at all, *because we don't let them be.*

But the more we strive—or intervene in our kid's lives—to keep them from failing, the more easily they will give up the responsibility to do things for themselves. It's sort of like dishes, at least in my household. If one person does the dishes all the time, the other person will simply let them pile up and never take on the chore.

When kids game, they often let all their responsibilities go by the wayside. Because you, their parent, are there, always running backup. "Did you do your homework?" "Did you study for your history test?" "Is your science project done?"

Let me offer you a karmic lens on this problem—another concept I learned from my time in India. Basically, the karma we sow determines the karma that we reap.

Let's look at what's being sown here. Your child is taking all the wrong actions, but what are the consequences? Are they late to school? No, because you have taken on the responsibility to get them there. Every time you do something they should be doing, you are cultivating a child who is dependent.

It's hard to let your child fail, especially when it's so easy for us to step in and help them succeed. It's natural that you would want to protect your child from reaping what they sow. That's what good parents do. But now, in the world of gaming addiction, doing the right thing as a parent can end up with the *wrong consequence*. You are enabling unhealthy gaming behavior by protecting your child from the unhealthy consequences of their own actions.

Why do we do this? Because failure costs them so much. You understand the costs of failure, far more than your child does. A single poor grade doesn't seem so bad, but they'll learn soon enough that it destroys the chance for the coveted high GPA. But now? They don't know that. And they won't understand that until later, when their grades are irreversible and they're applying for college.

What would happen if you stopped waking up your kids in the morning—assuming your child is a high schooler? Well, I'll bet they would be thrilled the first day. Maybe even okay the next day. But then, the next morning, they'd be handed their third tardy pass. In many schools, that's putting them at risk for suspension. Suddenly, this is on their record. What happens if you skip waking them up several more times? Now maybe they won't even be able to graduate. Oh, man, not go to college with their friends? Be stuck in the class below them?? Be the one kid who had to repeat freshman year???

Once things get very serious, and they realize it, then they'll start waking up on time. They might even ask for your help. And, most surprisingly, they'll actually *appreciate your help—instead of resent it.*

But if you keep cleaning up their messes—or forcing them to hold the broom while you micromanage the effort—they will never take responsibility back on their own shoulders.

If you want to move forward in this process, you can't have one party with all the freedom and one party with all the responsibility—that just doesn't work. We need shared responsibility—and shared power—which sometimes we parents are loath to give up. Parents I've worked with are reluctant to give up responsibility for good reason. As a parent, you are going to make better choices than your child—they could so easily screw up. The problem is that by the time they learn from their mistakes, parents fear it will be too late—the consequences will already be set in stone. But once you figure out how to relinquish some power, your child might finally learn to accept some responsibility.

Managing Your Emotions

When you sit down to talk to your kids about gaming, you probably try the usual tactics: You explain how important their development and behavior are for their future. You try to be encouraging and understanding, and you approach your child with kindness and support. But if you're being honest, what you are feeling is entirely different. You are likely feeling some amount of fear, frustration, and guilt. You're scared of what their future might look like, you're frustrated that you two are on different sides of this issue, and you feel guilty that you haven't been able to fix this already. If your child stays on this course, their life will be ruined!

The problem is, when you parent from a place of fear, frustration, and guilt, you will project those feelings right onto your kid. And children, as you've probably long since figured out, are incredibly emotionally perceptive. They notice that there is a discrepancy between what you are saying and what you are feeling.

What Happens When You Parent Out of Fear

What happens when you parent from a place of fear? Oftentimes, you try to manage your own fear by exerting control. For example, if you are afraid that your child may drink alcohol at a party, you may simply forbid them from going to the party. The fear is managed by shaping the environment. But that desire to control is stemming from a negative emotion. You know that if you control the circumstance, you will no longer be afraid. You might decide that you want to scare them straight, so you approach them with toughness—*This is going to ruin your life!*—and then you exert control. In essence, you are responding to your own fear by becoming overly controlling.

But when you exert control, your child is not on your team. Sure, you're no longer afraid, but what is their experience? They don't see the same danger you see—so the response feels disproportionate. You're each starting from a different set of assumptions. They feel controlled, and they resist you. They are going to be frustrated by your restriction, and they are going to empathically feel your fear. And how do they deal with negative emotion? They game.

Your fear, and your controlling response to your own fear, will send them right back to the game. When you are operating from a place of fear instead of a place of understanding or cooperation, you are going to end up taking steps backward.

What Happens When You Parent with Frustration

It's completely understandable and common to find yourself getting frustrated. You wish all your interactions were peaceful and loving, not angry and divisive, but, every day, things just keep getting explosive, right? Maybe you wish you could spend more time with your child, teach them to play chess or how to draw, or play tennis instead of seeing them engaging in gaming all afternoon, but you just don't have the time.

What happens when you're trying to parent when you're tired and frustrated? When we get frustrated or angry, we think in black and white, we blame others a lot, and we stop listening. In a moment like this, you might yell. You might punish. You might double down on love. But however you react, you want circumstances to immediately change to fix the problem. In response to your frustration, they'll get scared or they'll apologize, or maybe, just maybe, they will become compliant. But compliance isn't the same as being independently driven to change—they will depend on your anger to change, and you, in turn, will get the sense that the only way they'll ever listen to you is if you yell. This is a toxic cycle.

What Happens When You Parent with Guilt

As gaming negatively impacts your child's life, it is hard not to feel responsible for the problems they're facing.

But the truth of the matter is that the world you're raising your kids in is completely different from the world any generation in the history of humanity has ever raised kids in. The world is changing, and the challenges that you face are changing with it. You have nothing to feel guilty about here!

Let's start by understanding how guilt affects our behaviors. If your child is struggling, you will naturally try to help them. In the case of something like gaming addiction, you can try to help them, but sometimes the situation doesn't improve. Your child needed your help, and you are failing to provide it. This results in a feeling of guilt. This feeling will drive you to try again—you've let your child down, but you're not giving up. But since you're operating from a place of guilt, instead of a clear mind, you may be destined to fail again.

This is what we often see in the parents we work with—they try and try and try. As each failure piles up, eventually, the parents start to believe that things are hopeless, which is perfectly logical: If you try something five times and fail, why would you have any hope that the sixth time will be a success?

Parents start out feeling guilty, but, eventually, they withdraw out of sheer apathy. When you submit to this hopelessness, that is your brain telling you that there's no chance of success. When you feel hopeless, a part of you gives up, because your brain doesn't want to spend resources on something that has no chance of getting better. Hopelessness is the brain's way of keeping you from acting. If your child empathically absorbs that despair and hopelessness, anything you try to do to fix their gaming problem is doomed to fail.

Here's the bottom line: All of these responses are understandable! If you're afraid and exert control, if you get frustrated and angry and demand change, if you feel guilty and hopeless and decide to throw your hands in the air, if you stop listening and don't want to hear their side—all understandable. You are human, after all, and can't always control your emotions. But any action you take while you are so emotional—any boundary you set or consequence you mandate—will be inconsistent.

Why? Emotions don't last forever—by definition, they come and go. Any time you set up boundaries, limits, or behaviors relating to gaming that are driven by emotion, these will lead to inconsistency, because the energy you have to enforce those limits will shift as quickly as your emotions do. As your feelings change, the plans that you laid out will change as well.

My aim is to help you manage and decompress those emotions, to help you build an alliance with your child by developing a shared understanding and a set of common goals, based on consistent cooperation, not the whims or emotions of the parents or the child. A parent who is feeling frustrated, scared, and guilty will evoke, empathically, frustration, fear, and guilt in their child. These negative emotions simply lead to more gaming.

How to Avoid the Negative Emotion Trap

A key portion of my approach to coaching parents through this is helping them support their own emotions, so that they can work toward building a healthy dialogue with their child. After all, children will learn to recognize their emotional state—and how to manage their emotions—from their parents.

Part of the reason I have a coaching program for parents is to respond to this kind of blind spot. Some parents resist seeing it. "I don't need help. My kid is the one with the problem," they'll insist. To counter this resistance, I ask them to think about the kinds of circumstances their kids do well in, and what circumstances their kids tend to do poorly in.

When you see a household that has a kid who is struggling, it's very common to also discover that the parent of that kid is under a high level of stress. Perhaps a family member is having financial problems; maybe there is a divorce on the horizon, or someone in the household has lost their job.

Struggling or stressed parents often overlook their own need for recreation time to unwind or aren't focusing enough on their own physical health or diet. They might be super-stressed at work, or working too much, and, as a result of all these stressors, they might not be handling their own stress in a healthy manner—perhaps they're reaching for more than a glass of wine every night to wind down, or they are spending far too much time on their own phones.

To take control of the situation your child or your family is in, you need to take care of yourself first—that's the way to set your family up for success.

So, let's pause here to assess things. How do you feel about your life? Are you stressed out? Stretched too thin? Helping your child overcome their gaming addiction isn't about brief, intensive interventions. It is actually the opposite—real change will only come with small, incremental efforts that are sustained over time. To help them over the long haul, you need to be in a healthy place yourself so you can help your child get healthy over time.

I sometimes tell parents to think of it like this: If I'm sailing a boat, and I change my course by just one degree, after a year of traveling, I'll end up in a completely different place than if I hadn't made that slight course correction. That's our goal with problematic gaming and gaming addiction. Parents feel like this is a *huge problem to overcome*, and they are right.

But a huge problem doesn't require a huge solution—quite the opposite. Small changes over time—like the change of one degree in direction—make the biggest impact in the long run.

“

A huge problem doesn't require a huge solution—quite the opposite. Small changes over time—like the change of one degree in direction—make the biggest impact in the long run.

Make Your Own Game Plan

Our goal is for you to be calm, cool, and collected every time you have to deal with your child's gaming. So, I recommend self-care for parents that involves a lot of things you should be doing for your own happiness anyway.

- **Sleep:** We all know that we need to get enough sleep, but this bears repeating, because a well-rested parent is a parent who can help their child when they're going through something difficult, without their own emotions complicating the situation.
- **Emotional support:** Support can come from a variety of places—parents, siblings, spouses, and friends. That is, as long as they're offering the helpful sort of support. Are these people you are reaching out to actually supportive? Does it *help* when you talk to them? If not, you might want to seek advice from a different set of friends than you usually do.
- **Therapy:** This book isn't a replacement for therapy, either for you or for your children. But it's a great first step to start thinking about how you're doing, as an individual or as a family. It's never a bad idea to shift some stuff off your plate and seek professional help.

At the end of the day, the parent who is calm, cool, and collected does the best job both supporting their kids and setting limits with their kids. You don't need a whole lot—you just need to be able to be on your A-game when the time comes to confront your child's gaming.

Remember this: Taking care of yourself allows you the freedom and power to properly parent your child.

You need to better manage your emotions so you can better help your children manage theirs. You will learn not to give in to temper tantrums and cave. You will set yourself up for success by taking care of *you* first.

Now that you understand the neuroscience of gaming, and the psychological needs it is fulfilling for your kids, not to mention how your own emotions and habits come into play, you are prepared to take the next step. It is time to start talking to your child.

PART TWO

Talk

How to Talk to Your Gamer

Now it's time for action, but maybe not in the way you're thinking! Instead of starting in with limits, boundaries, and consequences, the first course of action is to talk to your child—truly talk to them. In order to understand what video gaming means to your child, you need to sit down and discuss the topic with them; then you will work to form an alliance so you can begin weaning them from problematic or addictive behavior.

The chapters in this section will help you assess your child's awareness of their gaming behavior, get on the same team on the issues, begin the vital process of connecting to one another when it comes to this critical topic, and then, finally, to begin laying the foundation for the boundaries you are likely itching to set.

CHAPTER 4

The Moment of Insight

Assessing Your Child's Readiness for Change

M ost of the parents who end up coming to me for help with their loved one's gaming habits have kids who are in their teenage years, maybe in high school or the early years of college. But video games are marketed to a wide range of player interests, and playing them can become problematic for people of all ages.

Generally speaking, though, the older the child or young adult, the more insight they tend to have about their gaming problem. With insight comes several stages of readiness for change. Let's take a closer look at what you can expect.

The Pre-Insight Phase

If your child is really young—say, under twelve—they are likely not very self-aware; they are unlikely to have put the pieces together to see that they are gaming too much. I call this the "pre-insight" stage of development. They just know that you're letting them play online, they like it, and they'd like to play more. This isn't a case of psychological denial; instead, it is simply because a child's brain (more specifically, their frontal lobe) isn't developed enough to think about their future.

This is the time when you, the parent, need to take the reins; you are the boss! They're young enough that you still provide a lot of structure for their day—you set their bedtime, you make their meals, and you likely organize their social lives. Therefore, you can and still should set firm limits on video gaming—how much time they can spend at it, where they must sit when gaming, and what games they are allowed to play. Compassion and validation should always be the first techniques you use to dismantle your child's resistance to change, but you may have to set firm boundaries without their initial buy-in. Try to be dispassionate with this task—set your boundaries without letting your emotions get involved.

What's important at this point in your child's life is that you set these limits and stick to them *consistently*. You're laying the foundation of good gaming habits with kids this age and you need to hold the line on the rules you've set for the family.

As your child becomes a late "tween" or young teenager—when they turn twelve or thirteen—things get a little trickier. You see your child physically starting to mature, and maybe they are also starting to be more insightful and articulate about school and friends. The biggest problem is that they *think* they know everything, but they don't. They don't know what they don't know yet. Their brains are still very much a work in progress and vulnerable to the pull of gaming. They are not yet able to understand that gaming could become problematic for them (it's still just fun!) or that it may already be problematic. They are still in the pre-insight stage of their young lives.

Stage Trumps Age

As your child becomes a full-fledged teenager, they will start to develop a strong sense of who they are. They'll feel like they're smart and competent, and they will begin to argue that they can make decisions for themselves. It's true that they are *becoming* aware at this stage—and it's reasonable to assume that they do have insight into the ways that gaming is interfering with their life. Indeed, they may already be at that *aha* moment, or what I call "post-insight." Even so, they are now teenagers, and teenagers will rebel against anything that you unilaterally impose on them. At this point, you have to start working *with* them, rather than against them.

Of course, your child's readiness to engage in conversation about their gaming or their acceptance of your rules for their gaming isn't always about age. Sometimes, you might have a very precocious adolescent who already knows that their gaming is a problem. You could also have a very oblivious adult ("man-child"—see the box on page 73) who is entirely unaware of his problem. Furthermore, your child might be in a very different place mentally than his best friend across town, even if they are in the same grade. My simple mantra is that *stage trumps age*. And, importantly, what is their *insight* into or *self-awareness* regarding their problem? How *ready* are they to change?

Sometimes it's tricky to figure out where your child is in the process of understanding or having insight into their gaming behavior. Oftentimes, children who are post-insight will appear to be pre-insight, primarily because they don't feel safe vocalizing their concerns. In their heads, they believe, "If I admit that there is a problem, the game gets taken away." They are afraid to give an inch, because they think you will take a mile.

The way to move from pre-insight to post-insight is to increase understanding.

You can't force understanding, but you can encourage it, usually through a combination of observation and open-ended questions, which we'll discuss in much more depth in chapter 6.

The Stages of Change

In psychology, we use something called the "stages of change" model to assess a person's readiness for understanding and making change in their life. There are five levels in this model: pre-contemplation, contemplation, preparation, action, and maintenance. For our purposes in this chapter, it's the first three levels of this model that are key.

Depending on where someone is in their cognitive readiness for change, the conversational technique you use to help them move toward it is critical. If you mismatch the technique with a person's stage of readiness, you can actually do more harm than good.

To bring this concept to life, consider the following example. I once worked with an executive I'll call Dave, whose son—let's call him Sean—had a problem with gaming. Dave rose to prominence in the executive world by being a problem solver. At home, he was a very loving and supportive father, but he felt that his age and life experience gave him insight into Sean's issue, as well as solutions he felt sure would fix it.

Dave tried to address things directly with Sean; he spoke clearly to his son about what he was sure Sean needed to do: cut back his playing to one hour a day, take at least two days a week off from gaming altogether, and apply for a job at a local summer camp, since Dave felt sure that Sean needed to spend more time outdoors.

Sean was receptive to all these directives—he was an agreeable kid, loved his dad, and wanted the tension to come down several notches between them; he was a willing participant in Dave's plan. But saying okay to the plan was a different thing from being able to carry it out—Sean tried, but, after a couple of days of cutting back to one hour of video gaming a day, his screen time started to creep back up again. He never did get to the "two days off a week" part of the program, and though he filled out an application for the camp, he never followed up and missed his chance to interview for a job there. For his part, Dave kept making new suggestions and adding directives to fix Sean's gaming behavior, but they went in circles; not only did the tension fail to dissipate, it ratcheted up.

The problem here was that Dave was not meeting Sean where he was at *cognitively*. Sean was willing to agree with his father's demands, but he wasn't cognitively ready to admit he had a big problem, so he kept falling short in his efforts. Sean's motivation came out of a desire to please his father, not out of an honest realization that he needed to change. His short-term obedience was admirable but destined to fail, because Sean was not yet taking responsibility for his actions.

No amount of direction—or power of will—from Dave could take the place of Sean's buy-in, his willingness to admit that he had a problem, and his readiness to tackle the problem head-on. Until the two, father and son, came to see the problem from the same side, until they became a team, they would never be able to overcome Sean's attraction to gaming.

What I hope to teach you in the coming pages is how to overcome these kinds of hurdles. What is your child actually ready for? How can you meet them where they are instead of dragging them to where you want them to be? You can develop a whole elaborate plan, with steps from A to Z, but if you're pulling your child toward you instead of meeting them where they're at, it's never going to work.

In chapter 10, and also in appendix A (page 265), I'll take you through a more detailed look at how to propel your child through the stages of change and lay out a concrete plan in terms of timing and specific things to say to move them along. But, for now, I just want you to understand and recognize the various stages of change.

> You can develop a whole elaborate plan,
> with steps from A to Z, but if you're pulling
> your child toward you instead of meeting
> them where they're at, it's never going
> to work.

The Pre-Contemplation Stage

In this cognitive stage, your child has a lack of awareness that there even is a problem with their gaming.

This is the pre-insight moment I outlined above—your child just isn't "there" yet, not ready to even contemplate a change. They might indeed have zero awareness, but more commonly their professed confusion over your perspective is a defense mechanism at work.

Defense mechanisms usually sound like straight-up denial—denying the problem even exists—but some kids will also attempt to intellectualize the issue. "No, Mom, I don't have a problem because . . ." "I'm in control of my gaming . . ." "It'll become a problem when . . ." They will justify the problem, rationalize away the concerns, but there are always some holes in their argument.

In this pre-contemplation phase, your goal should be to ask open-ended questions to get them to *nonjudgmentally* view their own behavior and get them thinking. If you are judgmental, it will activate their defense mechanisms. So, instead, invite them to think through the behavior—both the pros and cons.

An open-ended question means that instead of telling them that they have a problem, you ask a question that prompts them to explore the issue.

"What do you think about your gaming? What are some of the great things about gaming? What are some of the negative aspects of gaming?"

An open-ended question is not the same thing as a rhetorical question. "Don't you think that you'll have lots of problems if you game for five-plus hours every day?" Rhetorical questions are used to make a point, not elicit information. The purpose of open-ended questions is to learn—not make arguments. When you are asking your child a question, make sure it is based on genuine curiosity. They're the expert; not you. You're just here to learn.

The Contemplation Stage

This stage of development is characterized by ambivalence, or some amount of internal conflict. Your child knows they probably should do something about their gaming, but there is something keeping them from doing it. They acknowledge that gaming causes some problems, but it isn't *worth the effort to fix them.* In other words, they know there are upsides and downsides to their behavior but, on balance, they still think that change is overrated. This is where Sean was at cognitively.

A lot of parents (like Dave) misread ambivalence for change readiness, and then make a common mistake: They pounce! The second their child says something like "I guess this could be a problem," they jump into fix-it mode:

Good. Then let's stop playing.

I'm glad you finally understand.

And by the way I'm taking away your game because I love you. You know that, right?

Unfortunately—and you may have experienced this already—the "pounce" moment has the opposite effect from what you intend. Because now your child doesn't feel safe sharing their concerns, and, even worse, they might start to resist you more. If your child is in the contemplation phase, you want to take their side, perhaps sometimes even to an exaggerated extent: "Yeah, I understand that the game is causing you some problems with your schoolwork . . .

but it is a lot of fun, right?" The right move to make when your child is contemplative is to use *reflective listening* to send their beliefs right back at them.

When you say something like this, your child won't automatically clamp down and resist, because you're not pushing against them. There's nothing to push back on!

In fact, when approached like this, they'll often move in the right direction—"It is a lot of fun, *but school is important to me.*" In this scenario, the child has come to this important conclusion; you haven't had to introduce it for them. Often, when a child says something like "school is important to me," parents will get so excited that they'll jump right to pushing them to give up gaming. But instead—once again—just reflect back. "Wow, that sounds like a serious problem. On the one hand, school is important to you, but on the other hand, gaming is so much fun. How do you think we should tackle that?"

The Preparation Stage

Once your child concedes that gaming is holding them back from other things in life or is interfering with their grades or driving a wedge into the family dynamics, you've moved into a new stage of their readiness for change, but it's still not time to spring into action. If you skip the preparation necessary, you'll get lukewarm results and problems with follow-through.

Instead, now's the time to *involve your child in the solution; the right move is to give them a menu of choices, but let them pick which they'll try.*

When I work with someone who has an alcohol problem, I try to use this kind of approach. When someone is ready to get sober, I ask them, *What should we do next*? What solution do *they* think might work for them? Medication? Psychotherapy? Joining Alcoholics Anonymous? As a doctor, I know that if I jump in and give them the solution *I* want them to try, it is scientifically less likely to work. The patient will know intrinsically what feels like a better fit for them. Instead, offer a "menu" of options and let your child place their own "order." For instance:

> *Allow your child input and control over when they can play: "Do you think that gaming after your work is done would work well for you, or do you want to game for a set amount of time?"*

> *Give your child a choice on how often they can play: "Do you want to game for certain hours of the day or certain days of the week?"*

> *Add "healthy things" to their diet instead of just restricting the "junk food": "What activities do you want to add to your weekly schedule? Chess, martial arts, learning a musical instrument?"*

> *Focus on content instead of the amount of time spent on gaming: "Which specific games would you agree to cut out of your gaming instead of us restricting your hours?"*

Using a menu that your child can "order" from solidifies their involvement in the process and offers them a measure of control and ownership over the outcome. This leads to buy-in, and when it comes to children and changing behavior, buy-in is everything.

The Man-Child

In the eyes of the law in most countries, eighteen is the legal age of adulthood. As a practical matter, however, many eighteen- and nineteen-year-olds are still living at home (at least when they're home from college) and open-ended questions and menu options are still appropriate strategies to effect change in their behavior.

Once someone crosses the threshold of about twenty, however, they have to have a big say—indeed, be the driving force themselves—in whatever change needs to be made in their gaming life. Whether you're this person's parent, loved one, partner, or sibling, you can't really force them to do anything they don't want to do.

You are now in what I call the man-child zone. Of course, there are woman-children out there, too, but approximately 70 percent of people I work with who have a video game addiction are boys or men. The man-child might be a twenty-three-year-old who is living in his parents' basement and doesn't have a job. He is the age of an adult, but he doesn't actually behave like an adult. The man-child has, along the way, been developmentally stunted; he looks like an adult, but he behaves like a teenager.

The man-child problem is a challenging situation, but it isn't an impossible one. My guiding principle for all ages is that the worst thing that you can do for a person is anything that they can do for themselves. Irrespective of how old they are, if you're doing something for your kid that they can do for themselves, it's a problem.

Let's say you're living with your boyfriend, and he plays video games all day, so he doesn't do his own laundry and you're doing it for him—that's a problem. If your son or daughter is still living at home, and you've been cooking every meal for them, because that's what you've always done, it's time for a wake-up call, and it needs to be pretty harsh.

The first thing to do is to just stop what you've been doing to support them. Not all at once. Start with something small to begin the process of promoting independence. The goal eventually is to stop doing anything for them that they should be doing for themselves. Maybe you stop doing his laundry for him. Next up, you might stop cooking for him. Soon enough, you have to stop cleaning up after him. Let him do it. *Make* him do it.

No doubt about it, your adult-child is going to be frustrated by this tactic, which is why it's important to take these steps gradually. But if they *can* do it for themselves, they *should* do it for themselves. By doing all those things for them, you're basically encouraging them to remain a child.

By taking care of all of their needs, beyond allowing them to remain a child from a helplessness perspective, you are also enabling their gaming problem. If you do their laundry, cook their food, clean up after them, and perhaps allow them to live rent-free in your home, so they don't even need to hold down a job, you are creating an unstructured, wide-open, fertile environment for them to fill with as much gaming as they want.

But if you stop taking care of all their human, adult needs for them, what will happen? Well, they'll need to stop gaming, at least for a little while, if they want to eat or do a load of laundry. But that is progress, right there—one less hour of gaming a day, just so they can feed themselves and have clean clothes.

If you support them financially—by buying them games, filling their fridge, paying for their WiFi—this is also something you can cut back on. They'll have to stop gaming, eventually, in order to get to work, so they can fuel their habit, or even pay rent. Little by little, you want them to start fulfilling their adult responsibilities themselves. Once they begin to do so, you are helping them take their first steps into a post-insight world, one in which they can foresee a future in which they can actually stand on their own two feet.

Lights! Camera! Action!

After what's probably been a long period of arguing about their gaming, it'll definitely feel great to get to a place where your child has some insight into their behavior and has bought in to the idea of making some changes. Enjoy that first "win." But remember that now is not the time to press FAST-FORWARD—slow and steady is the way to go.

"Success" isn't the destination we are aiming for here; it is an ongoing process. The most important thing to remember is that you and your child are in this together. You are a team, and you'll have the most success if you manage to stick together. Now it's time to really form an alliance and to solidify your plans together.

CHAPTER 5

Building an Alliance

How to Get on the Same Team

The world is a dangerous place. But good parenting is not about preventing your child from experiencing it. After all, walking down the street can be dangerous, but your job as a parent isn't to keep them inside—it's to teach them how to walk down the street, to look both ways before they cross, to recognize danger and learn how to avoid it. You have to teach them how to protect themselves, because you won't always be there to do it for them.

As you can tell from the last few chapters, I strongly believe that the internet in general and video gaming in particular make it easier for kids to form relationships. But as we've discussed, sometimes the relationships our kids form online are with people we—and they— know precious little about. Without meeting these people in person, we can't rely on our instincts about their authenticity and whether they are a good or bad influence on our child. Now, we might hear an occasional voice over a computer speaker, but we don't really know anything about these people.

You can't change the internet and you can't keep it away from your child. All you can do is teach them how to be good human beings, to teach them to be concerned about who they hang out with. And if you can do that, you're going to create an exceptional kid.

The more you get involved in their life—and even in their online community—the better chance you will have to influence your child's life and protect them from other bad influences. To do this, your first task is to get on the same team as your kid—we call this "alliance building."

Shift the Dynamic

As I discussed in part one, many kids turn to video games to suppress negative emotions. This is why building a therapeutic alliance is so important. If you can learn to sit, listen, and talk to your child, then, ideally, they will come to you with their negative feelings, instead of venting or avoiding those feelings through gaming.

If, on the other hand, you are in a confrontational or verbally combative relationship with your child, they'll run *toward* their internet relationships and away from you. This will only further isolate them and lead to them cutting you out of their life. If you're worried about the bad relationships they seem to be forming, don't accidentally push them toward those relationships. You have to figure out how to be a counterpoint to those bad relationships by forming a good, healthy, strong one with your child.

So, let's start here. Ask yourself: *How do I forge a good relationship with my child again?*

When it comes to talking to your kids about video games, I am willing to bet that, as of right now, you can't have a conversation without it becoming an argument. You say one thing; they dig their heels in and insist on the opposite. Point. Counterpoint. No one ever wins these arguments. And even if you win, you lose.

Some of you who are reading this book are just starting to worry about the amount of time your child spends gaming. Others might already be worried about the tense relationship that exists between you and your child when it comes to this topic. Still other parents know there is a big problem. You've probably tried to do something about it, and you've been met with an unusual degree of resistance. You've tried to change something, and they're resisting that change.

No matter where you and your child are on this spectrum of gaming behavior, that is a dynamic that you need to step away from. Avoid making your relationship oppositional. You want them to do something, and they don't want to do it. So anytime you try to have a conversation with them, they're already going to start by thinking of you as the enemy. The inherent tension in that dynamic is going to activate the amygdala, the survival center of their brain—the part that triggers fear in order to protect them. If they think you're trying to take their video game away, they're going to respond with fear: They're going to become defensive, and they're going to resist you as a way to protect themselves.

When the amygdala is active, it causes us to think in terms of black and white. We stop seeing shades of gray entirely. Strangely enough, that's actually the way our brain is supposed to work. Thousands of years ago, when did human beings experience fear? Mainly in response to predators: Saber-toothed tigers. Crocodiles.

Snakes. You certainly don't want your brain to appreciate shades of gray in those situations! You don't want it to think about nuance: Hmm, I wonder if this is a friendly saber-toothed tiger? Perhaps that leopard has just eaten and isn't very hungry? Nope. Your brain just wants to protect you, so it wants you to act; the adrenaline-fueled fear response kicks in, and nuance goes out the window.

When this part of your child's brain is active—when they're in full fear response—they're never going to be receptive to what you have to say. Despite your attempts to communicate a lot of important information and endless love, nothing seems to work, right? Everything you try falls on deaf ears—and that's because your child's brain is literally tuning out and rejecting what you have to say. So "rightness" doesn't matter. You're black, they are white; there are zero shades of gray.

The more you can have a new kind of conversation with your child—where the goal is working toward understanding them better, rather than threatening to take the game away or complaining about their grades—the less likely they are to get defensive and shut down communication with you. Instead of an argument, you are aiming for understanding. Not just them understanding you, but you understanding them. Oftentimes, we explain to our child what they're doing wrong and expect them to change, but your child needs to have a voice if that change is really going to occur.

Once you have demonstrated to your child that you're willing to understand them, whatever you say next is going to carry much more weight.

Disarming Fear

My approach to building this kind of alliance starts with fear disarmament. If your child thinks that you're coming for the games, they'll fight you every step of the way. *Disarm their fear.* Toward this end, it's important to engage them with understanding. Opening lines like "I'm worried about how much you're playing games," "I don't like how much you're playing games," or "You're ruining your future" will only trigger their fear.

To flip the script to disarm your child's fear of losing something they cherish (gaming), try these conversation starters instead:

> *I want to sit down and talk to you a little bit about how much you play video games because I would like to understand it better.*

> *When I look at a video game, I see something that's kind of recreational. I know that you've enjoyed doing plenty of fun things in the past, but it really confuses me that you're playing so much, because I haven't seen you do something like this before.*

This kind of approach works well because you're stepping out of the role of the omniscient parent. You're admitting to them that you don't know something, and that you're seeking *their help* to understand it. That is likely completely different from your usual authoritarian stance: "I'm worried about you, and this is what you should do."

With this in mind, the first goal I have for you is to be able to have a conversation with your child about video games—and listen carefully, because this is the key!—*without it affecting their gaming.* They have to feel comfortable talking to you about gaming without being petrified that the conversation is going to end with you taking their console or computer away.

Most families go into these conversations as if it's some sort of battle, or maybe a contest. And the prize is basically how much the kid will get to play video games. If you really want to engage your kids, the first thing you have to do is just take the prize completely off the table. You must be able to have a conversation with them without having them think that anything they say is going to change how much you let them play.

"

If you really want to engage your kids, the first thing you have to do is just take the prize completely off the table. You must be able to have a conversation with them without having them think that anything they say is going to change how much you let them play.

To kick-start a nonjudgmental conversation, explain that a nonjudgmental conversation is exactly what you're after: "Nothing you tell me now will affect your screen time. There may be conversations about that in the future, and I'd love to have you be a part of the process of setting those limits when we get there, but this conversation has nothing to do with that. I have no goal right now except for understanding."

Your goal here is to try to be a good parent—which means preparing your child to succeed. But as a parent, your job is *also* to let your child have fun and do things that are important to them. Tell them this! Even if they don't believe you right away, they'll hear you, and they'll store this knowledge away for later.

In the first conversation, you want to emphasize that you want to understand games better. You want to know more about what they mean to your child, why they enjoy them so much. You can mention that in the past you've been judgmental and haven't really tried to understand your child. If you can authentically own that, it'll mean a lot to them. Apologizing up front for mistakes you've made is tremendously important for repairing relationships. You don't have to force it, but make sure you put it out there.

That sounds like a lot, but it won't be too hard to hit all the needed notes. Here's an example:

I've been worried about your gaming for some time—as I'm sure you've noticed. In the past, I've let my fear for you shape my actions, and I've been harsh in limit setting. What I haven't tried to do is really understand why you play video games, and what you like about them, and what it is like to be a kid nowadays. I'm sorry about that, and I'd like to learn. I'm still worried about some of your behavior, but I think we both need to understand each other better in order to move forward. While we're talking about this, I don't plan on changing any limits to your gaming. How do you feel about helping me understand the gaming world better?

What you're doing here is very important—and it's not just about what you're saying. In this moment, you are also *modeling the right behavior*. When you behave in a reactionary manner—cutting off the WiFi at 10:30 p.m. with no warning because you're pissed off or snatching the controller out of their hands when they disobey you— they'll behave impulsively as well; they will respond just as irrationally as you have acted.

When you approach the conversation this way, you're modeling the following things for your child:

- You are attempting to understand their point of view.
- You are apologizing for mistakes you have made, and you are accepting responsibility for those errors.
- You are laying a foundation for setting future boundaries, ones that will need to be adhered to.

Making a New Connection

If you're able to have a nonjudgmental conversation about gaming and get your child to tell you what it is that they love so much about it, push your luck just a bit and ask if they'll let you play with them. Even if it's not your thing at all—and you have no interest in it becoming your thing—sitting next to your child on the couch and participating in the world that means so much to them puts you on the same team.

If your child is into playing the piano or is on a swim team, I'm guessing you have attended many a piano recital or swim meet, because you want to support them working hard at a thing that they love. Now's the time to extend the same kind of support to gaming. Give this activity a chance—not because you equate it with these other, more socially acceptable activities, but because *they do*. They are working hard at a thing that they love, and you are trying to find a point of connection with your kid. Meeting them where they're at is one of the best ways to do so.

Of course, your child might not be all that enthusiastic about you joining them online. Part of their hesitancy could be coming from the fact that they worry about all the things you will encounter there that you won't like, including sexualized content and a toxic environment.

You can address that directly ahead of time, if you want. Ask your child if there is stuff or language in their gaming worlds that they think will make you uncomfortable (or make them uncomfortable to see or hear in your presence). Reassure them that as long as their safety isn't compromised, you will be neutral toward it. You're there to learn, not to judge.

Developing trust with your child will take time—not days, but possibly weeks, and consistency is key. I suggest that you try to devote about an hour a week to this kind of outreach. This isn't something you have to add to your schedule in any formal way, but do try to make an effort to stay present and available for it. Your child will start to feel more comfortable with this level of honesty and openness the more you show up in front of them ready to talk—and, most important, ready to listen.

Remember: No one builds an alliance with another person in a vacuum; you can't extend an olive branch just one time. If your initial outreach to your child about gaming to establish understanding went well, great. But your attempts to connect with your child are far from over; you have to keep making that same effort, over and over again. It's important to establish a pattern of *regular communication*; as with anything, practice makes perfect.

CHAPTER 6

Communication 101

Learning How to Connect with Your Child

As I mentioned in the last chapter, building an alliance—and trust—with your child takes time. And to repeat: I recommend trying to sit down and talk calmly and openly about gaming with your child for about an hour a week until you feel that trust building and growing. If you can't find that time or if you are making the time but the talks aren't going as you'd hoped—maybe these talks are painful for everyone involved, or you all continue to devolve into old communication patterns—you may need a refresher course on non-combative communication. In this chapter, I'm going to share with you some strategies that I know work.

The Four Techniques of Good Communication

One thing I learned in medical school is "Good diagnosis precedes good treatment." In other words, if you want to fix the way you talk to your child, you have to understand where the problem is. This isn't complicated—there are just four techniques to this kind of conversation that you need to internalize:

1. Open-Ended Questions
2. Reflective Listening
3. Expressing Confusion
4. Going Meta

Technique #1: Ask Open-Ended Questions

Earlier, when we worked on assessing whether your child had any insight yet into the ways in which gaming is interfering in their life, I touched on how important it is to use open-ended questions to help open lines of communication and gain back your child's trust. Now it's time to get a little more advanced in your understanding of a good open-ended question and gain confidence in your ability to use this technique.

Open-ended questions don't elicit yes or no answers, nor are they leading. A true open-ended question might be something as simple as: "What do you enjoy about gaming?" Notice that something this simple has a powerful anatomy in that it does not mention punishment and therefore does not trigger the fear response from your child (which would make them shut things down quickly). The fear that surrounds boundary setting (taking consoles away, turning off the internet) precludes fruitful conversations from ever starting.

Notice, too, that this question asks a child for help in

understanding—it gives them the power to teach us something, for once. Think about what's going on there. A lot of what we do as parents is to try to teach our children what's right and what's wrong. We've been doing that since they were born, basically. Oddly enough, what we find, especially as kids get older, is that if we try to teach them something, they become resistant. But if we can *help them figure something out for themselves*, that's where the magic happens. Open-ended questions do this.

Open-ended questions tend to *create distance* in a way that helps a child feel safe in responding. In addiction psychiatry, we often use distance to talk about hard things. Instead of asking a kid directly, "Do you smoke pot?" I might ask a much less direct question, offering them some distance from the discomfort: "Does anyone at your school smoke pot?" This way, you're opening up a line of communication without being accusatory. The same goes for these conversations about gaming.

Good open-ended questions also lack *judgment*. If you start the conversation off by implying that you think that they play too much—that's a judgment. Instead, you want to ask them to help you understand what it is that attracts them to the game. Here are some good open-ended icebreakers:

What do you like about games?

What is a "gamer"?

What's it like to grow up with video games everywhere?

What kinds of games do your friends play?

And on to more sensitive topics:

> *Do any of your friends struggle with gaming too much? What's that like for them?*

> *If you struggled with games, would you feel comfortable telling us? What could we do to help you feel more comfortable?*

> *What do we do that makes it hard for you to talk to us?*

In response to these kinds of questions, you're likely to hear something along the lines of: "I play games because it's fun. And right now I'm young. I'm supposed to work when I'm twenty years old or whatever, but right now, I'm supposed to have fun."

Resist the temptation to respond with fury or firepower. Telling them they're already too old to *just* care about fun won't do you any good. Instead, a good response at this stage would be to validate the good point they've just made, then try to draw them out further on the topic. Consider saying something like: "I get that. Right now, you're fifteen years old and, yes, I want you to have fun. I'm kind of curious, what makes video games so much fun?"

That is a response that changes the dynamic. You're not telling them they're wrong, or they're bad, or they're dumb. You're using open-ended questions to get them to open up, not shut down.

Here are more open-ended and open-minded questions to try out during your conversations with your child. Don't try to cram them all into one session—use them over the course of several weeks. It is important for your conversations to develop organically and deepen as you go—there are no shortcuts to learning to communicate better with your child!

General Questions

These questions help invite insight into their gaming:

> *What do you enjoy about video games?*
>
> *What makes games fun?*
>
> *When do you have the most fun with gaming?*
>
> *Is the fun pretty consistent or does it change?*
>
> *Can you tell me about epic moments you've had in gaming?*

Big Picture

These questions help you understand their values:

> *What are you excited about?*
>
> *How do you envision your life going forward?*
>
> *What's important to you in life?*

Self-Esteem

These questions delve more deeply into their self-identity:

> *Do you identify as a gamer? What does that mean? Help me understand what a "gamer" is?*

How do you feel about yourself?

Do you struggle with particular things?

Online Community

These questions will help you get a better sense of who is in their online world:

Who do you play games with online?

Do you talk to them when you're not playing games?

Can you tell me more about them? What do they do? Are they working?

Do they have families?

Are they your age? Are they in college?

What are they interested in?

Intersection of Gaming and Real Life

These questions will help your child examine their place in the world:

How do "gamers" perform in society?

What is the relationship between gaming and real life?

What do you think about school, extracurricular activities, etc.?

What kind of challenges do you face?

What makes those challenges hard to deal with?

What kind of support do you think you need for those challenges?

What do you think about how much you play?

Gaming and Relationships

These questions will help your child open up about their social network:

Do your friends play?

What's it like having friends who play games?

What does your significant other think about gaming?

Do any of your friends have problems with gaming? How do you know?

If you're able to engage your child in conversation using some of the questions above, you might then also be able to probe a little further and more directly into the pros and cons of their online life and relationships. You might ask: Do your online friends ever say things that make you feel uncomfortable? Do you ever worry about the people you hang out with or get concerned about the things they say?

You can ask more pointed questions, and you can delve into deeper issues, but reserve your judgment. Remember that you are here to connect with your child and learn more about this part of their world, not lecture them about how to live their life.

Technique #2: Practice Reflective Listening for Emotional Validation

To keep moving in this healthy direction, not only do you need to think about how to ask good questions, but you also have to invite them to explain themselves to you without fear of judgment. How? By using reflective listening. When we use too many open-ended questions in a row, it feels like an interrogation. To avoid that, we're going to mix in "reflective statements"—which should encourage your child to open up more.

Reflective listening is a very simple technique, but we humans are often terrible at it. It goes like this: Whatever your child says to you, just repeat it back. I know that sounds weird—it's not normally what we do in conversation. Usually, if you're having a conversation with someone, they say something that prompts you to respond to what they just said. For instance, maybe they share their opinion, then you share yours: "My favorite color is red." "Really? My favorite color is blue!"

When the substance of a conversation is a little heavier than color preferences, arguments often ensue. Point counterpoint. Devil's advocate. Reverse psychology. Whatever you want to call it, we're basically psychologically wired to do this. But we have to break this habit to demonstrate reflective listening.

Again, this sounds fairly basic in principle, but reflective listening is challenging in practice precisely because it's not what we're programmed to do. When someone expresses a negative emotion to us, most people tend to want to either problem-solve or reassure the other person. This urge is magnified when the speaker is your child. Consider this: Your daughter comes to you and says, "Mom, I'm so

94

hideous. Everyone hates me. I'll be alone for the rest of my life."
Your first response would likely be to jump right in and tell her,
"No, you're beautiful. You'll find love. You're so lovable. I love you
so much."

There's nothing wrong with this impulse to reassure or make
things better—it's a generous and loving reaction. But it's also not
meeting your child where they're at. What you're actually explaining
to them in that moment is that their feelings (of being ugly or unlovable, in the example above) are *wrong*, and that is very invalidating.
We need to help them validate their emotions and feelings, not ne-
gate them, even if we don't agree with them.

Think again about a different response to this scenario of a
daughter who feels ugly and unlovable. Using reflective listening, it
would go more like this:

YOUR DAUGHTER: Mom, I'm so hideous. Everyone hates me.
I'll be alone for the rest of my life.
DEFAULT RESPONSE: No, you're not ugly, everyone likes you,
you won't be alone.

Reassuring, but not validating.

REFLECTIVE LISTENING: I'm hearing that you feel
unattractive, that you're afraid you'll be alone, and that people
dislike you. You must feel terribly isolated.

Oftentimes, they'll respond after that. You can also follow up
with an open-ended question, being careful to avoid "why" questions: "What is making you feel so isolated?"

Notice that this parent is simply reflecting back what they are hearing. Then, if they could follow that reflective listening with an open-ended question, they might have a chance to get this girl talking: "Can you help me understand why you feel so ugly and unlovable?"

Now let's look at an example of a conversation about gaming. Perhaps you've asked an open-ended question about their gaming:

YOU: What do you enjoy about video games?

Your child might not get specific (yet) and simply give you a blanket answer:

YOUR CHILD: I love playing games, and I want to play games all day long.

Your instinct in this moment will likely be to correct or judge them, something like:

YOU: Well, I think that's really bad for you.

But what happened there? They stated their point, and then you took the counterpoint, so you both have created that oppositional dynamic that has gotten you and your child into conversational trouble before.

The reflective listening response would look like this:

YOUR CHILD: I want to play video games all day long.
YOU: Hmm, it sounds like all you want to do is play video games.

Notice that you've given them nothing to argue about, because you are just repeating exactly what they just told you. So keep at it.

YOUR CHILD: I like playing video games because I think school is boring.
YOU: Hmm. Sounds like school is really boring to you. And you find games more intellectually challenging, is that right?

Here's another example:

YOUR CHILD: Nothing besides gaming is really fun.
YOU: Wow, it seems like a lot of stuff outside gaming is really boring for you.

It can feel like you need to say more at this point, but you don't always need to. If you keep going like this, just listening and reflecting back what you hear to your child, a subtle thing starts to happen: Your child starts to feel heard, they feel understood, and they feel that you care. This is called "emotional validation." The more they feel this way, the more the fear center in their brain—the amygdala—shuts down. There's nothing to be fearful about, right? You're not fighting them or threatening them. You're not on opposite sides of the table anymore. You're on the same team, because you get it. The more you do this, the more validated they'll feel, and the more likely they'll be to listen when you speak.

Technique #3: Expressing Confusion

Once you have been working on your open-ended questions and reflective listening for a few weeks, you can move on to the next step: expressing confusion. As parents, you know that, a lot of the time, your kid will say things that don't make sense or are flat-out wrong. Our temptation is to tell them so right away. Of course you want to correct your child—you want to tell them that what they are saying doesn't make any sense, that they are wrong. But that doesn't work. It will invite resistance and, as you probably have experienced, they're just going to argue with you.

To avoid this kind of breakdown in communication, try expressing confusion instead. Point out the problems with their thinking without attacking them.

I use this technique in my practice when I'm working with someone with an addiction. If the problem is drinking, I'll start the conversation like this:

> **ME:** People in your life seem to be concerned with your drinking.
> **PATIENT:** No, it's really not a problem.

Instead of arguing with them, I'll express confusion and ask another question that includes zero judgment or opposition.

> **ME:** Okay, so help me understand, what brings you here?
> **PATIENT:** There are some problems at home; my wife is upset with me. And I'm having some problems at work.

ME: Okay, what are the problems at work?
PATIENT: My boss thinks I have a drinking problem.

Here is where I will express confusion again.

ME: I'm super confused. If you don't have a problem, why do all these people in your life think you have a problem? And if you don't have a problem, what are we doing here in my office?

In this case, expressing confusion will lead to my patient starting to share more details, more examples of what other people have observed in them. Now we have some concrete issues to discuss.

Let's extend this analogy to gaming. When your child offers you an excuse or explanation that doesn't make any sense or is just plain wrong, don't fight them on it. First, give them a chance to explain it. Frame your response to these kinds of false or nonsensical statements as: I'm confused. Often, when pressed, they'll come up with an answer that doesn't hold water. If it's a bad answer, you can make it clear that you're confused by it.

Showing your confusion and asking for a better understanding are tools I file under "disarming their defensiveness." That is, they continue to see that you're not punishing them, you're not taking anything away—you're just trying to understand better.

YOUR CHILD: All I want to do is play games.
YOU: Okay, I understand that all you want to do is play games right now. How about what comes next, after high school?

What are you doing here? You're reflectively listening and inviting their thoughts on the matter at hand.

YOUR CHILD: I'm going to go to college.
YOU: What kind of college do you want to go to? What do you think your chances are of getting in?
YOUR CHILD: I'm not worried. It'll be fine. I'll figure it out.

This is a common defensive technique—they won't acknowledge problems with their logic even when they know what they're saying makes no sense. Here is where you can start to express a little confusion. You're not opposing them, but you can push for a little more clarification.

YOU: It'll all work out? How is it going to work out? I'm a little worried about it, but you don't seem worried at all. I'm missing something. Can you explain how?

This is important: Don't be accusatory—you have to answer as if you are genuinely confused. Maybe they do have a plan, but you just don't know about it yet.

YOUR CHILD: I'll figure it out later.

Also important: Don't hammer away at them too much. When you express confusion in this manner, often your point is made pretty quickly.

YOU: What do you mean it's going to work out? How are you going to figure it out?

If they don't have any answer, your point has been made.

Remember, the goal of this kind of conversational style is to disarm their defensiveness. You're just trying to get them to talk to you. Because as long as they're not talking to you, they're not going to listen to anything you say.

Instead, when you express confusion, you are genuinely trying to understand their point of view, and to get them to explain it to you. You're demonstrating what you think and what you believe, and you are asking them to examine the holes in their own argument.

Technique #4: Going Meta

Talking about gaming with your children is difficult. As we've discussed, your child is often aware that they might have a problem, or that things aren't going so great, but they're reluctant to admit it. The child is trying very hard not to think about it or talk about it. If you try to push them into admitting it, you'll encounter a lot of resistance.

This is where things get confusing, because you know there's a problem and you're amazed and concerned they don't see that there's a problem. Why? Because they are working extremely hard *not* to see it. So either your child avoids every conversation about gaming, or every conversation goes around in circles.

So how can you talk about sensitive things without your child retreating into themselves? Take a step back from the specifics of the touchy subject; go to a higher level—go "meta."

When going meta, you don't want to get into the weeds or details—going meta is not about the content of conversations. Going meta is all about noticing a *pattern* of communication, rather than worrying only about the substance of the communication.

When you are going meta, you want to use a lot of "noticing" language:

> *Hey, have you noticed that it's hard for us to have a conversation about gaming?*

> *Have you noticed that you leave the room every time I bring up video games?*

The process of going meta is also a great opportunity to turn the flashlight back on yourself.

> *Have you noticed that every time we talk, I always turn the conversation into how I think gaming is ruining your life?*

Then follow up that observation with a good open-ended question:

> *What's that like for you when I'm constantly talking about gaming?*

You'll find that it's really powerful to start noticing—and naming—the pattern of antagonism or opposition in your relationship. This can open up opportunities to communicate because you're edging around the sensitive part—you're not probing it, you're just trying to understand why it's so sensitive.

Sometimes when there's a lot of tension between you and your child and you can't find a way to immediately fix it, the human temptation is to just avoid the issue that's causing the tension. When you "go meta," you don't try to fix what you are arguing about, but instead think about how you can rise above it and just observe the tension from the outside.

There's no judgment implied here. We aren't trying to press a button to fix everything—Hey, you shouldn't be frustrated with me, or I shouldn't be frustrated with you! We're just accepting the situation as it is and noting it.

Whatever the content of the conversation, the point is to rise just one level above it and comment on the *pattern of conversation* instead. At first it might seem that you are going backward in connection and conversational collaboration, but going meta allows you to target the issue of resistance. After all, sometimes conversations stall out when both parties think they are "right." When you get to that point, the conversation doesn't move forward, and neither side learns a whole lot.

Going meta allows you to approach difficult topics from a safe distance. Going meta also allows you to look at the pattern of communication and work on that, as opposed to picking away at a particular point that tends to always cause an argument.

Going meta allows you to be vulnerable and gives your child an opportunity to be vulnerable back. You've stumbled—both of you have. Neither of you is good at this, and that's great to acknowledge and will help you move forward. You're going to have to learn how to do this together, even if neither of you really has a clue as to what you're doing.

Vulnerability also allows us to model learning: Neither of us has all the answers. But we're in this together. We are lost right now, but we're going to find the answers, and we're going to figure it out together.

Dig Deeper to Discover

Let's assume you've been working on asking open-ended questions and practicing reflective listening for a few weeks—perhaps you've now had a decent conversation with your child about gaming two or three whole weekends in a row. What's been happening is that you have started to gain back your child's trust. They have come to trust that any conversation you two have about gaming is not going to automatically turn into conflict, restriction, or punishment, and they have started to open up to you. It might take a few weeks, or it might take a few months. It's okay to slow down the process if it's taking longer than you thought. Just give it some time, stay consistent, and keep seizing opportunities to talk with your child. If you keep showing up for them, willing to learn and willing to listen, they will eventually open up.

Once they have, you can start to lean in even further and start gently probing for more. Now's the time to ask some of the bigger questions you want to get to the bottom of, for instance, concerning the downside of gaming:

Are there any downsides that you see with gaming?

What makes those downsides hard to deal with?

Probing gently in this way has two major positive outcomes. First, you'll discover what really matters to your child, and it's long been proven that when we align addiction or problematic behavior treatment with what matters to a child, we have a far greater chance at success in treating the worrisome behavior.

Second, your child's answers to these deeper questions will likely reveal which aspects of gaming are the most important to them. This is vital, because once you are ready to start restricting gaming, you can begin by cutting out the things that will lead to the least resistance. Then, you can progress from there into the things that will be far more difficult for them to give up. Knowing ahead of time the paths of least and most resistance will certainly be helpful then.

By the end of several of these deeper conversations, you want to come away with the following understandings about your child:

- What matters to them—both their goals and their values?
- How do games bring them joy?
- How does gaming affect their friendships?
- What is the least enjoyable part of gaming for them?
- And last, but far from least, what are the potential concerns they may have about their own gaming?

Until you understand all these things about your child, you are not ready to start setting up boundaries. If you push ahead and start instituting restrictions without really understanding your child or what is important to them, this usually leads to failure. Even if you succeed, it often comes at the cost of your relationship with your child. If, instead, you've learned how to get on the same team as your child, and learned how to communicate better with them, you have a much, much higher chance of success when it comes to changing their gaming behavior.

Start Offering Them Something Better

Earlier in the book, we talked about how video games offer your kid intellectual engagement and challenge, which is something they may not be getting much in real life. Indeed, many kids who get deeply involved in gaming are quite smart—they learn things quickly and get bored with moving at the speed of their class average. Games also give them a sense of agency, a sense of power. They are the ones who control what happens in the game, and that is seductive, because most teenagers don't have much control over their lives. It's not their choice whether they go to school or where they live, but in a video game, they control the character—actually, they control the whole world. How do you compete with that?

I've mentioned that I have a number of patients with alcohol problems. As I work with them to curb their problem behavior, I'm well aware that I have to think about how to evoke a competing interest. Addictive substances give pleasure and take away pain. How do you ask someone to get rid of something that gives them joy *and* removes the bad stuff? It's really hard. But for people who successfully overcome addictions, it's not about willpower; it's about having a good enough reason to quit.

For my alcoholic patients, it's not enough to say, "You're going to get pancreatitis and get stuck in the hospital, or you're going to get liver cancer and need a transplant or else you'll die." Scare tactics like that rarely work.

Instead, it often requires rationalizing things to them through a lens or topic they care deeply about. "Your marriage is falling apart. Do you want to do something about that?" Or "Your kids are frightened of you. Do you want your kids to ever feel comfortable with you again?" Once we start targeting something that the person *actually cares about*, we have something with which to fight against the addiction.

One gamer I know told me he started enjoying games when he was about eight years old. I asked him what else he remembers happening when he was eight. He remembered doing math worksheets, something to do with addition. He'd do a worksheet, and when he finished, he would walk up to the front of the classroom to hand it in to the teacher. "What's next?" he asked. The teacher told him that was it for the day. He could sit and wait for the others to finish, and they'd go over the answers in about fifteen minutes, she said. So, the next day rolled around, and they did another worksheet. Again, he finished it in ten minutes, gave it back, and asked what's next? The teacher told him the same thing—we're still doing addition, just sit at your desk quietly and wait.

You won't be surprised that this kid started to get bored. Talking to him really made it click for me—schools move at the pace of the slowest child in the class, which can be terribly frustrating for a smart kid.

Video games, however, move at the pace of the person playing them. When you master one level, you don't have to wait until next week to go to level two. Level two is *right there, ready for you*. And that is incredibly satisfying! But if you keep failing a level, not to worry—you can just keep trying again. You aren't going to get left behind.

In other words, gaming fulfills an important need for children—a level of engagement that is meeting them where they are at. As a parent, you're going to need to help your child understand why they need to quit gaming. They need to understand what the cost of their gaming behavior is. But you also need to help them understand how to build something in their life that is greater, and more rewarding, than what they get from gaming. You need to help them find something that challenges them in the way that they need.

Oftentimes, we try to provide them with the "right" answers. College! A high GPA! Great extracurriculars! Volunteer work! But the drive to quit gaming cannot come from you; it has to come from them. Because they might not fully understand the consequences of their behavior yet, they may be obedient and agree with you, as Sean did with his father, but that doesn't mean they're on your side. They might be a good soldier, but they are not yet your ally.

You can't hand them a reason, because then it's your reason, not theirs. But if you can help them develop their *own* reason to quit gaming, they stand a very good chance of becoming a healthy gamer.

I recently had a patient who was a sophomore in high school, but school simply wasn't sufficiently challenging for him. He was fascinated by technology, specifically the use of AI—something that was just emerging at the time. So his parents and I suggested an internship at an AI tech start-up near his hometown. No surprise—he was into the idea and, when he got the internship, he loved going there. There he was surrounded by incredibly smart people who gave him a chance to show off his own smarts, too; he was finally feeling stimulated. Notice, though, that we didn't conjure the idea out of thin air—we asked about what excited him, and he said AI was fascinating; we ran with *his* interest.

Algebra wasn't doing it for this kid. But this new environment was. If your child is bored with school, how can you engage them in something that dovetails with their intellect? What are the things they're interested in?

"

> If your child is bored with school, how can you engage them in something that dovetails with their intellect? What are the things they're interested in?

Sometimes kids who are super into gaming can't think of anything that interests them more than video games. This actually happens more than you might think, so take heart if *I can't think of anything* is the response you get. Don't fall into the trap of providing answers if they can't think of anything themselves. Use your open-ended questioning skill set here: Ask them what it is like to have almost no outside interests aside from gaming. Listen to their answer, because this could be an important moment of insight into what's going on (or not) in their life.

As you talk with your child about their lack of interests, encourage them to remember back to what it felt like to have outside interests. What sorts of things did they once enjoy, and what made those things enjoyable at the time? We're after feelings now, not specifics—what sorts of feelings did that interest once evoke? Perhaps that will help identify a feeling that is currently missing and give you both ideas of how to try to find it again.

You can come at this question from a slightly different angle or with different vocabulary; think a little bit outside of the box.

What do you think is cool?

What excites you?

What do you think is wrong with the world today?

This line of questioning tends to work especially well with teenagers, because they are quite adept at pointing out everything that's wrong with the world—they probably have strong opinions about government, corporations, the environment, and certainly your parenting style. If you ask them what needs to change in the world, you might just get an earful, which is wonderful—you've moved their thinking from pretty exclusively about an artificial online world to the real world.

The next step is to ask them what they think they can do about the problems they've identified. Ask them how they think they could get involved. This question is important because *it puts the heavy lifting on them* (which is related to the "dumping it in their lap" tactic; more on that soon).

Don't come up with answers for them; engage them about what they're interested in, then the two of you can figure out together how to get them more involved. If they're really stuck, you can ask if they want your help. This strategy helps them understand that the real world is not a place where they are powerless and have no agency, but a place where they can make a difference. The more you have these kinds of conversations, the more you'll pull your child out of the virtual world and into the real world.

Your Turn to Talk

Once you've done your best to create the sense that you and your child are on the same team, it's your kid's turn to listen. There's no need to rush this part—you need to be sure that your child is feeling heard and seen before you start in on your point of view. As discussed, it is a good sign that they are indeed feeling heard and trusting of your confidence when they start to talk to you again. Are you having repeated—though not always consecutive; there will be stops and starts—and decent conversations over the course of the month or more you have been working at this? If so, that is great news.

When you both are ready for this next phase, take the opportunity to thank your child for working with you so well thus far. First, they opened up to you by telling you what is important to them. Next, ask them if they are willing to listen to some things that are important to *you*. In other words, now that they are feeling listened to, ask them if they're ready to listen to what you're saying now. If you've done the first part of this alliance building well, they will be willing and ready to listen to your point of view at this point.

Above all, you want to get across the point that you'd like to work *together* to meet their needs, to find solutions that will help you both stop arguing about their gaming. Start by reminding your child that you are the parent(s), and that, as a parent, you have a multitude of responsibilities, and the first one on the list is preparing them for real life.

As best you can, try to align your responsibilities closely with their values, as we discussed in the last section. If, for instance, you learned earlier that they feel respected for their gaming prowess, layer that information into what you have to say about your own goals as a parent. Perhaps something like this: "It seems like the respect of your peers is important to you. I value that, too, and I think there are a lot of things that I would encourage you to do that will move you toward that goal."

Next, lay out other key *values* that you hold. Talk a little about what is important to you—such as a sense of community, a strong family connection, or a measure of personal success. Invite them to ask questions, so that they can try to understand you a little better. Stop your list occasionally to ask them what they think about what you are sharing.

Here is a quick rundown of what you're trying to achieve at this point:

- Explaining to your child—with them agreeing with you, preferably—that there are certain things that need to get done, and you can come up with that list together.
- Reminding your child that your goal is not to take things away. Explain that you might have done that in the past, but only because you were *trying to achieve a particular goal.*
- Making clear that you would prefer if you two were working together toward a shared goal; you don't want to institute changes unilaterally.

- Last, you'll want to have clearly stated your hope that you two will work toward figuring out ways to move toward fulfilling their basic obligations as a child/adolescent/adult while *minimizing* the cost to them. Getting them to verbally agree that this is important is very helpful.

Here is some sample dialogue to get you started:

YOU: Hey, thank you. I really appreciate that we've been talking over the last month. I've been trying to learn from you, and I feel like I understand this stuff way better now. I think I understand now that the reason that you want to play games is because of X, Y, and Z. Is that right?

YOU: Now I have some thoughts I'd like to share. Are you ready to hear them? Can I tell you my thoughts?

Wait for them to say yes. If you've been doing a good job building an alliance, it should be hard for them to say no to a question like this. Now it's your turn to share.

YOU: Here are the values that I think are important: X, Y, and Z. I know you care about spending time with your friends. I also think that having a healthy social life is really important. My concern is that there's a little bit of a difference between gaming all the time with your friends and having a healthy social life.

YOU: I know you have told me that you're sort of reluctant to do X, Y, or Z. (For example, go for a walk in the woods, go play in the park nearby, join the chess club, etc.) What I'm trying to think about is what can we do to help you become more socially comfortable and, at the same time, not cut out your current gaming friends.

Dump It in Their Lap

The net result of all this talk—you listening and validating them and them listening to you—should be that you'll have isolated at least one common goal. Maybe it's just something simple like *We both want to stop arguing about gaming rules.* Or perhaps you can agree that reengaging with friends in real life is something to work on. Whatever the goal, you want to make sure your child feels as if they are going to be a vital part of the process. The best way to do this is to get them to figure out a solution for themselves. Yes, I'm serious. It's actually a very effective strategy—I call it "dumping it in their lap."

Because most parents are inherent problem solvers, your child has likely not had to do much in the past to achieve their goals. When your child wanted to learn to play the piano, you found them a piano teacher and signed them up for lessons and drove them there. Same with pretty much any extracurricular activity, right? Now that they are getting older, and especially when it comes to their gaming interests, you need to work with their desire for independence (which is one thing they dearly want, and that gaming has given them a sense of) and foster it in a real way. You're going to have to stop solving all their problems for them!

My goal is to help your child become independent and regulate their own gaming behavior. A big part of engendering their own independence is to let them come up with their own solutions.

Parents are often not very good at this. Frequently, if kids do poorly in school, the parents will jump to take on the responsibility of helping them achieve success. Here is an example of something that definitely happened in my house when I was a kid, probably more than once. I would tell my parents that I had an art project due the following day, even though it had been assigned two weeks earlier. In a state of last-minute panic, I would tell my parents that I needed art supplies. My parents, wanting to protect me from failure, dropped everything they were doing at the eleventh hour, and we'd run out to get art supplies. They would help me finish the project two hours after bedtime, and we'd all wake up the next morning exhausted. Maybe something like this has happened in your household, too.

Think carefully, though. In this scenario, what behaviors were my parents reinforcing?

- That there is a lack of consequences for my own mistakes or procrastination.
- That telling my parents things at the last minute is acceptable.
- That they will always drop everything to solve my problems.

You can drop a problem in your child's lap by simply asking a few questions.

YOU: When was this project assigned?
YOUR CHILD: Two weeks ago.
YOU: I'm curious why you chose not to tell me before now.
YOUR CHILD: I forgot.
YOU: How much notice do you think is reasonable for me to go get you the supplies you need for a school project?

What can you do to remember that window of time better next time?

What will your plan look like when you receive the next assignment?

How are you going to stick with this plan in the future?

Think about this same strategy when it comes to checking homework. Many parents want to check homework nightly, so they put their own needs and responsibilities on a back burner to check the homework as soon as their child says it's ready for review. Instead, put that important responsibility back on them.

> *I get home at 5 p.m., and I have to start cooking at 6. Dinner is at 7, and then we're done cleaning up around 8:30. It is important for me to be able to check your work—since that's what we agreed on. When should I do that? We've said that you can start playing after your work is complete and checked. So it sounds like I can check it at 5:15 p.m. every day, and you can start playing at 5:30. What if it isn't done at 5:15? Then the next window to check it is at 8:30. Understood?*

The key here is *not* to accept responsibility for "making things work"—don't do all the negotiating and accommodation. Instead, *dump it in their lap.*

> *I'm not available to check things on Saturday morning—if you want to play on Saturday, what can you do to make sure your work is done on time on Friday?*

Once you and your child have agreed on a shared goal or skill you both would like for them to attain, you can leave it up to them, as it were. Dump it in their lap. Yes—just tell them they have to figure out how to accomplish it, and you'll look forward to their suggestions for reaching that goal when they are ready to update you.

> *What is a realistic plan for you to maintain a B average? Can you think about it, then lay out all the steps so I can understand it clearly?*

This may seem like a lot, but if you think about it, you're tapping into one thing that gamers are really good at. If you give a gamer structure, they are excellent at figuring out solutions within that structure. In a video game, the rules of the game are set; gamers have to be very creative in order to figure out solutions within that game's rules. Help your child succeed by tapping into that gamer brain. There is no wiggle room in the rules of the game, because that's how the game is coded. But if you give them some amount of latitude within the structure they've been handed, it gives them the option to move the pieces around—within reason—to get to what they want. Dumping it in their lap fosters independence and offers them a sense of ownership for finding a solution that works for them.

Trust me. "Here is the goal. You figure out how to make it happen" is often far more effective than you trying to impose a particular solution (yours) on them. In this way, you are teaching them that they have the requisite skills to solve a problem themselves—they don't need you to do it for them. They will hear what you're saying—

you don't have to do it my way, it just needs to get done—and feel a sense of ownership over the process.

> **"**
>
> You are teaching them that they have the requisite skills to solve a problem themselves—they don't need you to do it for them.

I know that ceding control over solution creation might not come easily to most parents. I get it—you are likely feeling very impatient to see real change in your child's behavior, and you probably have a very clear idea of the quickest solutions. Holding your tongue—keeping your great ideas to yourself—is hard to do. But it's critical. Patience is a virtue, after all! Your child won't change because you've asked them to, and they are more likely to effect lasting change if they "own" the solutions.

Don't press them for an immediate update on their ideas for solutions to meet your shared goal. It's reasonable to ask for an expected timeline—*When do you want to talk again about the solutions you've come up with?* But understand that brainstorming and iterating on a solution process might take more than a few hours. Give them a couple of days to think about it, but don't wait too long. Within a week of agreeing to the goal, you want to have a clear strategy to try.

Waiting for your child to come up with solutions, however, is no reason to abandon the very good and meaningful work you've done up to this point. The strategies you've learned in this chapter, continuing to ask open-ended questions and to practice reflective listening, will serve you well as you move into the next phase of course-correcting your child's gaming habits: laying the foundation for setting and keeping boundaries.

CHAPTER 7

Laying the Foundation for Boundaries

Creating Structure in Your Child's Life

At this point, you've learned so much—about the games themselves, what they do to our kids' brains, and how they fulfill many of their needs. You've learned about yourself—why you're struggling and how to help yourself to help your kids. You've learned how to talk to your child about video games and figured out how to start getting on the same team. And you have learned to listen to your child and, hopefully, they are starting to understand better where you're coming from, too.

But at some point, enough is enough when it comes to conversation. All parents ask me the same fundamental question: How do I get my kid off his damn screen? In other words, when do I get to lay down the law?

We're almost there! Indeed, part three goes into detail about how to set and maintain boundaries. But you still have a little more pre-boundary work to do so that when you get to that important stage, you'll have a solid foundation from which to build.

Creating Structure

An unstructured life is fertile soil for getting addicted to video games.

Think of it this way: People who play video games tend to procrastinate a lot, so if they don't have some kind of set structure, the video game is just going to fill that time. Some of the people I work with are in their twenties. They spent too much time gaming while in college, but as soon as they finished college, things went from bad to worse. Without the structure of their academic lives, they no longer had anything anchoring them to the normal rhythms of life; suddenly they could play for fifty or seventy or even a hundred hours a week.

One of the most important things you can do for your child is to implement a sense of structure, within their days and around their lives. I appreciate that this goes a little against the grain of what I've been saying about fostering independence in your gamer, and indeed it's reasonable to start to be a little more hands-off as your kid gets older. After all, when you have a seventeen-year-old, you're a lot more likely to ask them if they did their math homework and believe them if they say yes. They're seventeen, not seven, so they have more responsibility and more control over their time. And they should! But if your child has a problem with the amount of time and energy they put into video gaming, chances are you're going to have to treat them a little bit more like they're seven instead of seventeen, and really work with them to set up structure in their lives.

Of course, structure is not always easy to implement. Kids are smart, and many kids are sneaky. One family I worked with thought they had their son's out-of-control gaming problem solved when they decided to try to create physical structures and barriers around his gaming habit. They moved the PlayStation console to their living room so they could monitor daytime play, and then when they went to bed at night, they locked up the power cord in their liquor cabinet and took the key with them to their room.

Maybe you can guess what happened next. Their son watched YouTube to teach himself how to pick a lock. Once he had that trick mastered, he snuck downstairs each night, picked the lock on the liquor cabinet, and plugged in his beloved PlayStation. Many nights he'd play there in the living room until five in the morning. Then he would lock up the power cord again and go to sleep! Not surprisingly, his parents were finding it very difficult to wake him up in the morning for school, because he was only sleeping two to three hours a night.

One night, however, this tricky boy's sister couldn't sleep and went downstairs to get a glass of water in the middle of the night, only to stumble on her brother at his console. She ratted him out to their parents. They didn't have the problem solved. Not at all. The real issue here was that the structure this boy's parents imposed on his playing was just a boundary—they never built an alliance to start with. This is why it's so important to build an alliance before we even start talking about boundaries.

If there is no alliance, you aren't on the same side of the battle. You're fighting a war, and it pits you against your child. And just as in any battle, every time you impose a limit, they are going to try to find a way to get around it.

The other problem with this attempt at boundary setting is that it was put in place to prohibit or discipline his access to his games, and that's it. The parents were thinking about structure, but they did so one-dimensionally. A better way to think about structure is not as a function of discipline, per se, but as a function of *planning*.

Let's look at the ways you can plan and set the family up for success, starting with yourself.

Start by Developing Your Own Structure

Start by looking at your own life's structure. If your life is unstructured, it'll be impossible to structure your family's life. You can't reasonably ask your child to be done with their homework every day "by the time you get home" if you don't come home at more or less the same time every day. If your schedule is unpredictable, you can't link theirs to it and expect them to be consistent. An unstructured household—or a disorganized parent—is one of the biggest risk factors for uncontrolled gaming.

You can't expect anyone to follow your lead if you're not leading well. You know this from other efforts you've made in your family: If you want to set an example for your kids to sleep regularly, to eat regularly, to prioritize family time at regular intervals, you have to do these things yourself! When you start thinking about boundary setting, you are going to have to operate within the structure that already exists. So start to become aware of your family's schedule, then begin to track it carefully.

Toward this end, consider the following questions:

How structured are your days?

What is the structure of your family unit?

Do you all tend to get up at the same time?

Do you connect at a certain time, or does every person sort of just fend for themselves and catch up when they can?

Do you all eat any meals together, and, if so, at what time?

You don't have to be perfect, and a little flexibility is important, but aligning everyone's expectations around a set schedule is a great first step at increasing the structure in all of your lives. Now, instead of telling your child that you want them to stop gaming and start their homework at a certain time, you can make sure that the "certain time" is one that works for the family and one that you'll be around to monitor.

Structuring Access to Games

We've all been told not to watch TV or work on our laptops in bed, lest we screw up our sleep schedule. But these days—especially since not so long ago, Covid made every school into an occasionally online one—it seems as if every kid can sneak in video game time while pretending to write their English essay. Therefore, it's important for you to help your child separate their work environment from their gaming one.

When you think about how best to structure your child's physical gaming access, here are some things to consider:

Where does your child actually play games?

Do they have a TV or console in their room?

Is their PlayStation downstairs in the living room?

If you set a gaming curfew of 11 p.m., but they have a Play-Station and TV in their bedroom, what happens after you fall asleep?

What do you do if your kid needs to do schoolwork on a computer?

Now make some changes. Studies show that if you move video games to communal spaces instead of bedrooms, you can reduce gaming time by about 33–50 percent. If you can organize things in your home so that your child does their homework on one screen and games on another, you can effectively limit sneaky game playing while pretending to do homework!

Even if you can't physically separate work from play this way, you can set different logins for work and play, which will help you monitor the amount of time your child is spending on gaming. You could also arrange for them to do their schoolwork outside the location in which they usually game. Perhaps they could go to the library after school and you could have them stay there until all their homework is done.

The important takeaway here is to get them out of their gaming environment, both mentally and physically. I find that this suggestion also works well for college students. I recommend that they leave their dorm room or their apartment to go study at the library. Once they've finished their work, they can return home to game.

If access to a library or study space isn't an option for your family, see if you can just convince your kid to use a different room in the house to do their homework, one where they wouldn't usually be gaming. Once they're finished, they and their computer can move back to their usual gaming spot.

Of course, your children may find a way to work through any physical or technical barriers—as in the liquor cabinet example above—which is why I'm so focused on alliance building and having your clever child working with you instead of against you. At the same time, understand that your child doesn't have a fully developed brain yet, so they aren't able to control their impulses. That is why you need to structure things in a way that can help them succeed.

Structuring Access to Content

There are a few key things you can do when it comes to trying to police the *what* of your kids' gaming—that is, the kinds of games they are playing:

- Encourage your child to focus on multiplayer games on consoles—in other words, having friends over and playing something together can be healthier than internet play.
- Use parental controls to set limits on certain applications or games on the computer or console. Screen-time app

limits on phones or computers, as well as enforced "downtime" limits, during school or after bedtime, are useful for helping kids understand how much time they are spending on a certain game or app.

- Use parental controls on consoles or PCs to limit your child's access to certain kinds of games or language. This is especially useful for younger kids.

These limits are important tools to integrate into an alliance. Ideally, you have a plan in place for boundaries, and technology safeguards are an additional set of "guardrails" to ensure good behavior. They're supplemental—not primary.

Structuring the Timing of Access

Structuring the time your child can have access to games is another thing to consider. For instance, many gamers have a "Let's play one more" mentality that can keep them glued to the screen until well past midnight, if you let them. Indeed, it's estimated that a third of high schoolers regularly stay up past midnight during the week— and most parents I know are not able to outlast them, or their late bedtimes, to ensure they aren't staying up late gaming. (Firewall settings are a big help with this.) If you restrict internet access during certain hours of the day, you can reduce the kind of multiplayer gaming behavior that gets out of control.

The dream scenario is your child coming home from school and getting their homework and their chores done right away, and only gaming once they've met those responsibilities. But that's not always how it works. As you know, once kids start playing video games, it's awfully hard to get them to stop. But if you only allow gaming when everything important has been completed, you'll find that kids start getting pretty damn resourceful. They will be highly motivated to do whatever they need to get done so that they can turn on that console and have the chance to play for however long they have before you insist that they shut things down. If hustling to get their homework and chores done allows them a whole extra hour of gaming, you'll be surprised at how efficient they'll get!

If your child resists sitting down to do their work right away— for example, if they tell you that they want to come home and relax for a couple of hours, then get going on their work—you need to figure out if your child is capable of sticking to a plan before agreeing to it.

For instance, at 5 p.m., when you ask your child to turn off the game and start on their chores or the essay they need to write, are they able to quit on cue? If not, make some changes to this dysfunctional routine. Maybe offer them the option to relax after school, but without a screen. Then, try to push the game as late in the day as possible. Offer incentives for accomplishing the tasks on your agreed-upon to-do list before access to screens is granted. Games should be a positive reward, one you can both feel good about because the necessary stuff has already been taken care of.

Last, consider the fact that your child might get unlimited access *at someone else's house*. While you can't control what other parents allow and other families tolerate, you can put limits on when your child is allowed to go hang out at the house where you suspect there are warm and loving but slightly hands-off parents at the helm.

Utilize the Outdoors

We know that a main reason kids play games has to do with their mood and their anxiety, because when they're playing the game, they don't have to act a certain way, which alleviates uncomfortable feelings like sadness or anxiety. We also know that the more time your child spends around games, the more the games will colonize their mind. Any kind of physical distance from their consoles will help decolonize their mind. So, next, we're going to talk about getting your kid out of the house.

Studies have shown that being in the same room as your cell phone increases levels of cortisol—our primary stress hormone. Even if your phone is on silent mode, on a table across the room, you are more stressed than you would be if the phone were in another room. Even if you aren't using it, some part of your brain is thinking about it. This kind of mental work is scientifically proven to fatigue the brain. Mental fatigue makes it harder to focus on school and work, because focusing requires some amount of willpower. Bottom line: Electronics are basically a constant willpower drain.

It's therefore not enough to just have the console turned off; you need to get your child out of the house, physically away from their tech. You need to get them outside, where they'll find all sorts of benefits. In medical school, I learned that our calves are considered our "second heart"—any time we contract our calf muscles, they automatically pump blood back up the body. Walking improves cerebral blood flow, which helps remove waste chemicals from the brain, many of which predispose us to unhealthy coping mechanisms like drug abuse and gaming.

Sunlight itself has tons of positive effects. First, it regulates our circadian rhythm; exposure to sunlight during the day will help us feel tired at night. In addition, vitamin D is produced through sun exposure; vitamin D has a protective effect against depression and also increases energy levels.

There's some fascinating research about what happens to humans when they spend more time in nature. It turns out that plants secrete compounds called aerosols; when you smell a plant, these chemical compounds actually reduce anxiety and positively affect your mood. If your kids can smell the outdoors, some of the issues they use gaming to cope with will become less problematic. Lower depression and anxiety will mean less need to game. So, don't discount the power of the great outdoors!

Try to get your child outside at least on a daily basis. Ideally, you want to work your way up—start small, and little by little, work up to at least five hours a week, and eventually far more. This is the kind of small intervention that is going to have cascading, positive effects on reducing their gaming.

Not too long ago, we announced a new challenge to our Healthy Gamer community—we called it the Touch Grass challenge. We challenged gamers on the internet to spend more time outdoors. It was a one-month photo challenge where they could accumulate points by taking pictures of themselves doing things outdoors, like meditating in a park, going swimming, or picking fruit. Over ten thousand people from 118 countries participated.

We carefully measured participants' activities as well as how they felt about what they were up to. We asked them if they were having fun doing these non-gaming things. Overwhelmingly, they said yes.

We also asked if they were still able to hang out with their gaming buddies throughout the challenge. Again, they said yes, which showed that reducing their gaming time didn't impact the community of friends they'd built online.

Last, we asked if they wished they'd been gaming instead of spending more time outdoors. Here they overwhelmingly said no—which was a wonderful and important marker of the challenge's success.

The big-picture upshot was that harmful gaming behavior was reduced, in some cases significantly. The participants still continued to play games, but they were able to play games and then step away from them before their gaming became problematic.

Kids seem to love gaming in a dark room—how can you get your child to open the window shades, literally and metaphorically?

Start by going outside *with* them. Try scheduling more family time outdoors—take the dog on an easy hike, or shoot some hoops in the driveway, or take a bike ride to go get ice cream. If those options seem way out of reach, see if you can set up a study area or hang-out spot for your child near a window, where they will at least reap some benefits by being able to see trees or greenery outside.

Even a half-hour walk every day together as a family will have major transformative effects over time. Remember: If you change course by one degree, ten hours later or ten days later, you will be in a completely different place.

PART THREE

Act

Acting on What You Now Know

You are finally ready to formulate and institute boundaries. But let me warn you—as soon as you start doing this, you're going to run into resistance. Therefore, in part three, we are going to follow these steps. In chapter 8, we will go through the anatomy of a good boundary plan—everything you need to know in order to start formulating one.

Chapter 9 will then help you formulate a plan and work through it with your child, getting you to a point you both agree with, even if, at this point, neither of you will be perfectly happy with it. But agreeing on a path forward together is a big step—a vitally important one—and it means you are moving in the right direction.

The process of finalizing your boundary plan, however, necessarily involves engaging with your child to understand what matters to them and what they value—this plan is one made by *both* of you. If, at this stage, you run into some trouble agreeing on a plan, chapter 10 will help you learn how to deal with the resistance you will inevitably encounter, as well as address the common boundary-enforcing pitfalls I hear about all the time.

Even if you have done everything "right" so far, resistance from your child is basically a given when you are trying to institute new boundaries. If you want to skip ahead to read this chapter first, just so you're properly prepared for the pushback, feel free! Or else just read on, and maybe dog-ear it once you get to it. Resistance will rear up, again and again—but you will get better and better at understanding it and rolling with it.

The primary concern of part three is how to get your child to listen to you. We can talk for hours about good boundary planning, but if they aren't listening, it is never going to work. If you follow these steps and learn to engage your child in the process, setting and enforcing boundaries will get easier over time.

CHAPTER 8

The Components of a
Good Boundary Plan

B oundary setting is one of the most important tools in your
toolbox when it comes to helping your child have a healthier
relationship with video gaming. But it's important to remember that
boundaries are mile markers, not finish lines. The key to this part of
the program is making sure that you have defined these markers well
in the first place so you don't have to keep going back on what you
said, or recalibrating what your child will agree to. Toward this end,
you need to understand the components of a solid plan and understand how to manage the expectations—yours and your child's—
around its formulation.

Starting Small

How many boundaries around gaming in your home have you set in
the past few weeks or months, let alone years? And how many of

them have you failed to follow through on or let lapse in the face of your child's resistance or even *good* behavior?

To state the obvious, when you fail to enforce the boundaries you set, or when you let them fall by the wayside because "things are going in the right direction," you teach your kids that your boundaries are permeable and there to be stepped over or, one day, ignored entirely. This dynamic is damaging to both your relationship and, of course, the goal of getting them to play video games less often!

"

Boundaries are mile markers, not finish lines. Define these markers well in the first place so you don't have to keep going back on what you said, or recalibrating what your child will agree to.

Often, the problem is that your goals are too ambitious. They're not goals, they're wish lists, and they aren't reasonable in the least. My advice: Start small so that you can begin racking up wins. Instead of "Straight As in school, getting to bed on time, dinner as a family every night"—perhaps your wildest dreams—consider *what is possible* in the near term.

Think of this in weight-loss terms. You don't lose fifty-five pounds all at once. The healthy route is slow and steady, one pound at a time, one week at a time. Changes that lead to healthy and lasting out-comes are subtle and take place over the long term.

When it comes to setting realistic boundaries, I recommend what I call the "25 percent rule." For example, let's say your goal is to eat dinner as a family seven nights a week. That's a big goal, especially if right now you're eating dinner as a family exactly zero nights a week. Zero to seven isn't realistic in one giant leap, right? So, what's halfway between zero and seven? That would be 3.5 nights a week. Then take half of that—that leaves you with a little over two nights, if you round up.

Two family dinners a week is 25 percent of your desire to eat to-gether every night. With extracurricular activities and busy sched-ules, even two nights might be a challenge until it becomes a family habit or tradition. All the more reason to start small—maybe even rounding down to once a week, with a plan to ramp up to two times a week next month. I know this is the slow route, but it's also the sur-est way to meet your family dinner goals. And hitting this much more manageable goal will give you the needed confidence and mo-mentum to build up to several nights a week, which would be an unqualified "win" for everyone.

Likewise, the 25 percent rule is your friend when it comes to changing your child's behavior relating to gaming. Let's say your child now plays about four hours of video games on weekdays, but you want to get the time down to one hour a day, no more. You and your child are on different poles, to say the least. So, start by asking for a 25 percent reduction in their gaming as the first boundary def-inition: They can now only play for three hours a day. This will feel like a big concession to them . . . and not enough change for you. But it's a start. With time and increasing boundaries—once you have a "win" on this first step—you'll get closer to your goal.

Consider Your Own Schedule

A boundary plan is a commitment—months, maybe even a year or so, of your time—so don't just consider boundary creation in the short term, or in the context of an ideal situation. Instead, think of yourself when you are at your most stressed, and try to imagine being able to enforce gaming boundaries in that state of mind.

Policing your child's video game usage is likely only one of your responsibilities—you probably also have other family commitments, a job, other children to care for, a house to take care of, dinner to get on the table. Things get even more complicated when you're a single parent or have a household where there are two working parents.

This is why you need to define boundaries that are aligned with your own schedule. If you have a lot of expectations in your boundary plan, you need to make sure that you have a lot of points of contact to make sure your child is doing those things. The more you have committed to monitoring, the more touch points—frequent small interactions throughout the day—you need to set up with your child in order to do that monitoring.

For instance, as we've said, if you ask your child to have their homework done by 5 p.m. every day, you need to be physically capable of checking said homework by 5 p.m. every day. If you tend to still be at the office then, or always in a gauntlet of virtual calls, or headed out for your evening workout, a 5 p.m. homework boundary is not a good idea for your family.

If 5 p.m. is important to you (perhaps you want homework done before dinner, or because you know that your child procrastinates or that their energy drops off soon thereafter), you might consider deputizing someone to do the homework checking for you—a grandparent or babysitter, perhaps. But my rule of thumb is that if you want to see change, it's best to share in the solution personally. Maybe you'll have to change *your* routine. Or maybe you'll have to reconsider the 5 p.m. rule.

What about boundaries when it comes to nighttime gaming? If you go to bed before your child, you have to think about how you handle boundaries after hours with them. If their gaming console is in their room, then it is going to be next to impossible to enforce a boundary of no games at night. Maybe you'll want to use monitoring software for your router—programs that monitor or limit internet use, such as IP monitoring or bandwidth monitoring—to help enforce your nighttime gaming boundaries.

But tread carefully here. If you choose to use technology to help enforce boundaries, you need to let your child know you are doing so, lest they discover it and try to out-tech you. Much like the child who picked the lock on the liquor cabinet to access his console in the middle of the night, establishing a boundary without engaging your child in the process will simply start an escalating war of deception. That's not the right kind of atmosphere you want in your house. Also, it's likely that if you start a tech war with your child, you will lose. Given this, maybe the nighttime boundary isn't the proverbial hill you want to die on if you can't realistically commit to enforcing it. Start smaller than that—maybe start by laying out a boundary that needs to be enforced during daytime hours.

Bottom line: Boundaries can only be enforced around points where your schedule allows. Establishing a boundary that you cannot enforce results in training your child to ignore your words. Start by taking stock of your own resources. What can you realistically enforce? Then lay the boundary for that.

Again, you want to teach your child—in ways big and small—that when you say something, you mean it. Once they understand that, they will start listening to you more. One of the best ways of doing that is to pick a considered boundary and reinforce it 100 percent of the time.

"

> Boundaries can only be enforced around points where your schedule allows. Establishing a boundary that you cannot enforce results in training your child to ignore your words. Start by taking stock of your own resources. What can you realistically enforce? Then lay the boundary for that.

Define the Levers of Power

The specificity we've been talking about thus far is really all about the *levers* that you can pull in defining, plotting, and then enforcing the boundaries plan. Needless to say, a successful, well-rounded boundary plan will have a lot of levers.

The first lever is the articulation of the boundary itself. There is no "wrong answer" here; it's just important to know what you're asking. Things to consider include:

- Which games are allowed?
- Is the hourly limit you impose a daily amount or a weekly amount?
- Is bingeing on weekends allowed?
- What about when they go to a friend's place, especially if that friend has very different rules?
- Are you delineating the time of play—i.e., restrictions before and after a certain time?
- Are you outlining the circumstances of play—i.e., before and after certain work is done?
- Are your boundaries unbounded by either time or circumstance, but just contingent on satisfying certain conditions? "You can play as much as you want, but you have to make sure you get a B+ or higher in science."

Second, what are the consequences of violating the boundary that's being set? You have to get specific here, because "no games" isn't a good consequence. Think expansively:

- If it's no games, then for what duration?
- It could be no new games or no new gaming purchases.
- No online play—they could play alone, but not in the larger community they usually do.

- No in-room gaming—the only gaming system gets moved to the living room, in full sight of the entire family.

Determine Your Performance Metrics

Performance metrics is just a fancy way of labeling the behaviors that signal that boundaries and target goals are being met.

Remember when your kids were little, and you were trying to rush them out the door to get to school on time? "Shoes on, jackets on, backpacks on, let's go!" And then a meltdown would ensue? Most pediatricians advise using a psychological trick to get little children to listen to parents by giving them a choice—or at least the sense of having one. Instead of barking a list of orders at your kid, they told us, try asking them if they want to put on their shoes first or put on their jacket first. At the end of the day, both of those things have to be worn, but the child gets the option of determining which one they want to put on first. They get to choose the order of things, which gives them a sense of autonomy, but in the end, the kid gets their act together to get out the door to go to school. Win-win.

The same process can apply to picking target behavior when it comes to gaming now that they are older. Work with your child, not against him. Come up with a plan of action together, not just defining the parameters, but also the order in which you'll approach them: "What kinds of grades do you think you should be maintaining?" Or, "It is important that you do some kind of physical activity, some amount of social activity, some amount of family involvement, and some amount of chores. What would you like to start with?"

These are some performance metrics that will help you determine whether your boundary plan is going well or poorly.

Is your child:

- Performing well academically
- Completing their chores
- Following an agreed-upon daily routine
- Taking part in family activities
- Exercising daily
- Participating socially
- Behaving well generally
- Being financially responsible

Depending on your child, you may want to start with only one target, or if you're both feeling ambitious, maybe one target in each of a couple of these categories.

And don't forget the 25 percent rule. If your child hasn't exercised since five-and-under soccer, setting a performance metric of running a 10K next weekend isn't a realistic option. Figure out where they are at, figure out where you want them to be, then do the math and set the agreed-upon goal around the 25 percent mark. When thinking about limits for gaming, most parents in our programs focus on what their kid *should* be doing. Instead, success comes from focusing on what they can *realistically start with*.

Establishing Milestones

Agreeing on specific performance metrics can help you establish milestones. Milestones are *planned* portions of the boundary plan, agreed upon ahead of time so that both parties know what to expect—and they are very important to ensure that the plan works.

For example, milestones can be baked-in prizes that your child can focus on while they are moving in the right direction.

Remember that your child's resistance will increase in proportion—or close—to the lack of structure you set. When your child feels as though they didn't see the consequence coming, you'll really hear about it! If they have something that they can anticipate, however, things will feel less unfair or arbitrary and they'll be better at regulating their behavior. So, any time you set a boundary with your child, you want to build in milestones for reevaluation of the boundary. Their resistance to the boundary will be lower if they know you are going to reevaluate (the sooner the better, from their point of view)—and if you stick to that promise.

To use an eating analogy, consider this: If you set a boundary that your child can never eat desserts again, it will be awfully difficult to enforce. If, instead, you set the boundary that they can't have sweets for one week *and* that you will reevaluate after a certain event (such as eating their vegetables for seven days), then your child will be much less resistant.

Milestone #1: Weekly Check-Ins

Once you've talked through and mostly agreed on performance metrics (as well as the parameters of the consequences when metrics aren't met), you'll need to set up a regular time to check in, just as you might with an employee undergoing a performance review. This will be in addition to the nightly quick check-ins to see how the day's work is looking and should be a more specific weekly (or so) check-in for you two to meet and discuss how things are going, big picture.

When you first started building an alliance with your child, your weekly discussions were mostly about learning. As you start to institute boundaries, these weekly check-ins will help you and your child evaluate how things are going: Are you moving in the right direction? Is your child frustrated? If so, what about? Are you happy with their progress? How can you adjust and continue to move forward?

As usual, follow the format you've been working on. First, discuss what's been going on—ask open-ended questions and use reflective listening to understand their perspective.

When you start doing your weekly check-ins, open with the following questions:

- How did this week go?
- What was hard for you?
- What did you like about the week?
- How was your gaming this week?
- How do you feel about your chores, academic work, etc.?

After they answer, reflect back what you heard. And remember to *listen*. They aren't right or wrong here—this is just their perspective. Don't fall into the trap of trying to convince them.

You should also share your own thoughts on how things are going—and ask your child what they heard or understood; if you've been doing a good job at reflective listening, they should have picked up on it! You can:

- Share your own experience.
- Share what you are proud of or what was difficult for you.

- Share what you think went well.
- Share what you think needs improvement.

Keep in mind that even though you need to be consistent with your boundary enforcement, not all plans are fixed in stone. You both are always learning, so you may need to adjust the plans as things evolve. You might adjust to make things more flexible—maybe even give your child more access to gaming. Or you might adjust to make things more stringent—usually when the boundaries you're setting aren't achieving results. Any time you make such an adjustment, however, you need to state it clearly so that your child doesn't interpret the change as you becoming more or less strict. Share your thinking, your reasoning, then make the change.

Milestone #2: Rewards

The second type of milestone to bake into your plan deals with rewards. What can your child expect if they do a "good job" for one month—i.e., your weekly check-ins are positive for four weeks in a row. What is the reward at three months?

If your child is like most, they will want their good-behavior or goal-achieving rewards to be game-related, e.g., more access, a new game, or some new kind of hardware. It would be a whole lot better to set a reward that is not game-related (candy is great—it's temporary, whereas a new game or console is permanent!), and it's important to remember that making everything about more or less access to gaming can actually *overvalue* the role of gaming. But let's say they have strongly suggested that a new computer should be on the table as a reward.

If things have been going pretty well in your talks about changing their behavior, you would be completely forgiven (and totally normal!) for not wanting to ruin this good thing by completely shutting down their request to get a new computer. Instead, use the strategies you've already learned.

Start by having an open-ended conversation.

Why do you want a new computer?

What's the urgency?

What can we expect regarding your grades and family participation after you get it? (Dump it in their lap.)

It's okay to add gaming time or hardware (a new console, a new game) as a reward, but help your child understand that whether you say yes or no to a new game or a new console is based on their behavior *starting today*. It's crucial to use this conversation to acknowledge that things are going very well, and you are very happy about that. If the reward is gaming-related—for example, that request for a new computer—you could discuss the possibility of shifting from an ownership model to an access model, where access to the new computer is going to be based on certain things. You can let them know that if they continue to do what they have been doing, then they will have access to the computer. Even this—what you and I would consider a reasonable arrangement—might upset your child. You need to have the capacity to tolerate rocking the boat; *you need to be okay with your child getting upset.*

Also keep in mind that gaming-related rewards can sometimes do more harm than good. If you let them play for one extra day as a reward, for instance, it can be very hard for them to stop playing the next day. But, once again, you will have agreed to the boundary beforehand, as well as the milestones along the way. Built-in milestones foster a sense of accomplishment and reward over a gradual period, without violating boundaries. Your child will learn to expect prizes along the way, based on conditions that were set when you were laying out the boundary plan together. (Sounds almost like a video game, doesn't it?)

You want to build reward milestones outside of gaming as well. Many parents understandably want to make academic performance part of the equation. Focusing on GPA at the end of the semester can seem like a really important goal, for instance, but it's also one that feels far away for a child. Have it both ways, and build on small milestones along the way. For example, if your child gets an A on a test, then they get one day of gaming on the weekend. (You will need to do some math to figure out how many tests they have in the semester and whether that can be a sustainable way of rewarding them.)

Another example of a milestone is that if they finish all their homework for the week by Thursday, then they can take the weekend off from schoolwork. They will still be expected to show up for mealtimes and chores, but if they have done all their schoolwork by Thursday, they can game on the weekends.

As always, make sure both the boundaries *and* the rewards are ones you are able to enforce.

Milestone #3: Negative Consequences

The third category of milestones is negative consequences. What happens if their grades continue to plummet? What does the progression of restriction on gaming look like? Negative consequences aren't really about punishment. Instead, they are like guardrails—there to help ensure that your child doesn't drive off the proverbial road.

When you discuss negative consequences with your child, make sure they understand this. Make it clear that you want to work together, very hard, to avoid these consequences. You are both committed to adapting and learning, to keep things moving in the right direction. At the same time, there are crucial things that your child needs to accomplish for their health and security for their future, hence the need for their consequences to be on the table.

The negative consequences you set are going to be highly dependent on the age of your child and on your ability to enforce them. With younger kids or young adolescents, you—the parent—can still institute negative consequences that have some bite to them, since you are likely still their sole mode of transportation. As children grow up and gain independence, negative consequence enforcement gets trickier.

Here are a few negative consequences that parents have found helpful:

- Decreasing gaming time.
- Decreasing access to a particular console (for example—no PC gaming, but party games on Nintendo Switch, played in person, are okay).

- More chores.
- No sleepovers; restricted social activity.
- Limited access to phones or, in the most drastic cases, removal of smartphones and going back to basic text/calling phones.
- Reducing access or blocking use of particular apps, websites, or social media.

Start Making Your Ideal Boundary Plan

Now that you have thought about performance metrics and milestones, it's time for you to think through your own version of a perfect boundary plan. You will solicit your child's thoughts on your ideal plan soon enough, but for now just take the opportunity to realistically think through your own challenges, such as your schedule and your abilities to enforce boundaries.

The key element here is that you want to set the rules of the game, *and* you want to give your child a path to success. Because, though it might not feel like it right now, they do want to succeed, just as much as you want them to. Make sure success is within reach for them as you set up a realistic plan.

“

You want to set the rules of the game and you want to give your child a path to success. Because though it might not feel like it right now, they do want to succeed, just as much as you want them to. Make sure success is within reach for them as you set up a realistic plan.

A big part of setting your boundary plan is to define what is completely unacceptable behavior. If your child is engaging in some of these behaviors, you might not be able to start restricting gaming without first establishing a shared alliance about what constitutes no longer acceptable behavior, to either of you. You also may need to engage professional help (see part four for more on cases in which you might need a professional therapist to get involved).

What's unacceptable is going to be highly individualized, but over the years I've seen some or all of the following show up in many family plans:

- Using abusive language.
- Breaking things.
- Throwing extreme temper tantrums.
- Making threats of self-harm when gaming is restricted.

Have a conversation with your child about what you find completely unacceptable, what you don't like, and what you appreciate in terms of their behavior. This comes back to setting and managing clear expectations.

Writing a Rough Draft

Now that we've looked at the parameters of boundaries and getting your child on board with setting some up, it's a good idea to craft an actual written plan with your child. You don't have to force them to sign it, as that could threaten your burgeoning alliance, and certainly doesn't guarantee compliance. But it's a good idea to have mutually agreed-upon expectations written down in one place to refer back to, in case anyone wavers or forgets.

Start by discussing your needs and goals—yours and, by extension, your child's. Some of these need to be absolutes—as in, they are absolutely nonnegotiable. But those are the minority. The majority *should* be negotiable—the child should be able to choose.

A friend of mine has a saying she uses with her kids all the time: *You guys have a voice, but not a vote.* That's useful to keep in mind here. You, the parent, are in charge—but that doesn't mean your children don't have a say in how their life looks. When you discuss potential boundaries with your child, make sure they genuinely feel they have a voice.

Remember: That's a key part of getting buy-in—they need to feel they have some say in the process. And the process is all about progress—you should not expect complete change right away. Right now, you are mostly looking for movement, an overall shift in a positive direction.

Here's a reminder of the things you will be documenting:

Try to understand what works best for them. Then, develop concrete plans with compliance in mind. And don't forget to consider your limitations. As we've discussed, do not set a boundary that you can't enforce. If you feel that homework needs to be checked before they can play, you need to be able to check it. If the boundary has been set but you can't commit to meeting it, how can you expect your child to do so?

Develop consequences for success and failure now—not when the proverbial sh*t starts to hit the fan. If they adhere to the boundary for one week, what do they get? What about one month? On the flip side, if they fail to adhere to the boundary, what happens? At what interval are we going to be checking? Are our metrics for success matching? Do we agree with each other about what *good* looks like?

Develop a plan for reevaluation. If things aren't working, when will you know it? If you need to change—if things feel too restrictive, or aren't restrictive enough—when will you initiate the new changes?

Start as small as you can. You can dream big, but you are starting small. You want to work on one or two goals, at most, so don't get greedy at the start. Figure out the tiniest hill that you're willing to die on. Then start there.

Developing a Boundary Plan—Part 1

We've covered a lot of ground in this chapter, so it's worth explicitly laying out the steps for all those who digest information better in list form. There are six key components to defining and setting good—workable—boundaries with a child who has an unhealthy relationship to gaming. Here's how to develop your plan:

STEP 1: START WITH THE 25 PERCENT RULE.
- Pick one or two things you want to work on. Think back to all the alliance building you've been doing, then take into account the values that both you and your child have listed as important.
- Make a list of unacceptable behaviors, if applicable.
- Think about what your goals are, then implement the 25 percent rule.

STEP 2: DETERMINE YOUR RESOURCES.
- Think about your own schedule and what you can realistically enforce.

STEP 3: DEFINE THE LEVERS OF POWER.
- Think through what levers you have access to, and which are the levers you are willing to pull.

STEP 4: ESTABLISH APPROPRIATE METRICS FOR PERFORMANCE.

- Think about what metrics you want to use to determine success or failure.
- Figure out the trigger points for tighter or looser enforcement.

STEP 5: ESTABLISH MILESTONES.

- Bake in the appropriate milestones.
- How will you know whether your strategy is working?
- Set up a weekly check-in to discuss things that are working and things that are not.

STEP 6: GET READY TO PRESENT YOUR PLAN.

- Make sure the plan is one you're happy with, but please note that it isn't final yet.
- This is your dream plan; next up, you have to get your child's buy-in.

CHAPTER 9

Engaging Your Child
in the Effort

Once you have fully thought through all the possible dimensions of the various boundaries you want to institute, and you have analyzed the different levers you have available to you, it's time to start discussing boundaries with your child. Essentially, you want to get them on board. Instead of just laying down the law, try to engage them in the effort alongside you.

Feel Free to Jump Ahead

You'll no doubt encounter some resistance through this process; maybe you already have! Chapter 10 will help you understand where that resistance is coming from, and how to offset it. You might even want to jump ahead and read that material now if you're already getting pushback from your child.

Don't be disingenuous here, either—if you come into this conversation with a firm plan and don't intend to be swayed, your child will know it and won't bother engaging. Be willing to listen, and maybe even compromise, as you discuss the need for new boundaries with them.

Once again, you're going to use all the techniques you've been practicing and probably getting good at: open-ended questions, reflective listening, and dumping it back in their lap to prepare them to come on board with the new boundary plan.

You've probably already asked a number of the following questions in your weeks-long campaign to open up the channels of communication with your child. Keep at it:

- What is the most important aspect of gaming for you?
- What do you really enjoy about gaming?
- What do you not want to miss out on?
- Do you want to play every day?
- Do you want to play when your friends are playing?
- Do you want to play on weekends when there are special events in your video game?

Remember: You are trying to learn what elements of gaming are most important to your child. This line of questioning will also help you form an alliance on a boundary plan, by giving them some say in the process, while also standing firm on other things.

You can play on the weekend with your friends, but during the week, can we agree that these tasks need to be done?

Then what comes next? You're going to listen to their answer and reflect their feelings and thoughts back to them. *Reflective listening!*

> *Okay, so it sounds like it's most important to you that you get to play when your friends are playing. I get that you don't want to get stuck only being allowed to play when all your friends aren't online.*

Validate their emotions, and try to understand their fears and concerns about these new boundaries being put in place.

Then it's time for you to weigh in:

> *Here's where I'm coming from. As your parent, it is my responsibility to make sure you do particular things. How can I encourage you to do these things, and yet still let you have fun, which is part of what being a kid is about?*

Or:

> *This original plan sounds great. What happens if you don't stick with it?*

What's this strategy called again? Ah, yes. *Dumping it in their lap!*

Offering Menu Options

Once you and your child have talked about the dimensions of boundaries, you want to *enlist your child in picking the right boundary.* Having their buy-in is incredibly important. Here again you'll ask open-ended questions about what they would consider a good boundary, and involve them in the decision-making process for assessing whether they are living within it and meeting the goals associated with it. Ideally, you'll select two or three options together, and then refine them.

I like to use a dinner menu analogy to illustrate how this conversation might go. Let's say you ask your child what they like to eat and they say, "carbs and meat." Nothing wrong with those options, of course, but you know you have to find a way to get something green on their plate, too. So, when it's time to discuss the dinner menu for the week, you might offer them the following ideas.

- Steak salad with garlic bread.
- Pulled pork sandwich with zucchini and carrots.
- Meatballs and pasta with a side salad, or veggies mixed in with the pasta—their choice.

YOU: You said you like carbs and meat, so those are the main things on the menu. But you need to eat some vegetables, too. If you prefer a salad before you dive in, we can do pasta and meatballs, and if you prefer not to have a separate thing, I can grate zucchini and carrots in with the pork. Which do you want?

In a conversation about gaming, it might go something like this:

YOU: What do you like about games?

YOUR CHILD: I like playing with my friends and the thrill of competitive games, especially when the most people are online, which is usually between 8 p.m. and 11 p.m.

YOU: As a parent, I need to make sure you get enough rest and that you do okay in school. You don't have to be at the top of your class, but your job as a kid is to learn *and have fun*. So here are some options:

- You have to finish all your homework and chores and have dinner with the family by 8 p.m. So no gaming when you get home. But if you get all that done, you can play until 10 p.m. on weeknights and midnight on Friday and Saturday.

- You say your friends like to stay up super late on weekends—that sounds fun, but that means you need to get all your stuff done Monday through Thursday. You can stay up until midnight on Thursday, Friday, and Saturday, and you can sleep in on Saturday and Sunday. But you need to get all your chores done during the week in order to sleep in. And then it's in bed by 10 p.m. from Sunday through Wednesday.

- I'm open to other suggestions, but the main thing is that the plan has to include adequate rest, adequate time for schoolwork, and adequate family involvement.

Adding Boundaries and Being Prepared to Pivot

Even as you and your child make progress toward agreeing on some initial boundaries, they might—at some point earlier than you'd hoped—be unwilling to talk about the full game plan, or they might be unwilling to accept new boundaries you want to institute in response to new, unacceptable gaming behavior. They might—understandably—respond to additional boundaries with dismay: "You're always adding more!"

Acknowledge that you do tend to always add more: "Yes, I am. What's your understanding of why I'm doing that? How does it feel for you to have me keep doing this?"

Offer them some control in the process they are finding frustrating. As a parent, it is important for you to try to slow the process down and ask them to reflect. What is their understanding of why you're setting these boundaries?

Focus on validating their feelings and talking to them about the reason you are tightening boundaries one after the other. Invite them to recall recent conversations you two had about shared values. Continue to return to those shared values—what are we moving toward here? See what they remember.

Then offer your explanation or interpretation: "Six weeks ago, when we talked about this, you said you were interested in X, so we are instituting this boundary to help get you there."

This is why the weekly check-in is absolutely vital. This is when you debrief. You can talk about what is or is not working. Make whatever decisions you want going forward, but limit any conversations about potential changes to the boundaries to this weekly check-in. In the moment, the limit continues to be enforced, but your child's needs can be addressed down the road. They will appreciate the knowledge that their voice is being heard and that you are interested in working with them.

They will learn that the weekly check-in is where they will get their needs met—that's how to get them to the table. Don't react, respond, or offer flexibility in the moment of enforcement; a reward or requested change to a boundary should only come when they come to you for the weekly check-in to discuss the matter in a calm moment.

Having a conversation about the idea of the "process of progress" will help. "It must be frustrating because it may feel like I'm punishing you for doing better. Is that what it feels like?" Then you can dump it in their lap: "Here is my challenge as a parent who loves you. I see you doing a fantastic job, and I also want you to be able to play games. I don't want to impose these ten boundaries on you at the same time. That feels unfair to me. Do you think it would be unfair if I did it all at once?" They will probably respond with, "Yes, it feels unfair."

You could respond with, "So I am stuck because I don't want to do it all at once because it feels unfair to you. It feels unfair to me, too. At the same time, all of these things need to happen. How can we make them happen?" You might be surprised to know that the number-one complaint that most recovering gamers have about their parents is that they aren't consistent enough with their discipline and that they let their children get away with too much.

Be transparent and share your problem and your shared goals with them. They may push back: "But I don't want all of those things. You are setting the bar too high. I think this should be enough." So, engage in a conversation with them about where the bar should be. "Okay, these are the seven things I wanted you to do. Can we do two more, and then sit down to talk about the remaining ones? Or maybe we only choose one of those. How do you feel about that?"

Children may also feel that just because you're starting with one, your continual addition of limits feels like a tightening noose. You want to acknowledge this as well—but invite your child to consider why you're doing this in the first place. They have two options in front of them—to game excessively, fall behind in life, and maybe eventually they will figure their life out (as I did). Or, with the two of you working together, you can create a life where they are happy with their physical appearance and levels of competence, have plenty of friends and appropriate social skills, and are progressing toward a career or academic success that they can take pride in. All while gaming. Which would they rather have?

But don't forget to learn as you go. If you create new boundaries in response to a goal breach, pay close attention to whether that works or not. If, for example, you learn that restricting after-school play but allowing late-evening gaming doesn't really impact your goals, because your child only wants to play during the late-evening hours anyway, it is useless to try to impose that particular restriction in the future.

Remember that the boundary or punishment that *induces the right behavior* is the one we want to go with.

Holistic versus Nitty-Gritty Boundary Setting—What Works for You?

Almost every parent I've ever consulted with about their child's video gaming wants to know what the healthy amount of gaming hours is for children. Or they'll ask the same question another way: "How much gaming is too much?"

I'm guessing you came to this book looking for answers to these questions as well. But as I said in the introduction, there is no universal *right* answer, because kids are unique. You know your child is a totally different person than the kid down the street. Likewise, technology addiction is highly individualized. No surprise: So are the solutions! Boundaries, therefore, need to be nuanced and keyed to your child's specific behavior.

Here's a common example of boundary definitions: "If you do your chores, you will get to play your game" or "If you do your homework, you get to play your game." However, this kind of unidirectional boundary setting can get you into trouble for a number of reasons. For example, you may not be able to check if your child has done their homework. You may not be able to check if they did their homework *properly*. Moreover, your kid might tell you whatever they think you want to hear to get access to the game.

Most parents will then try to get more specific:

- Two hours of video games on weekdays, four hours on weekends.
- In bed by 10 p.m. every night.
- Complete a full list of chores every day.
- Otherwise . . . Cue punishment.

But this very straightforward approach opens up a lot of problems as well, and, again, the child who has to live by these boundaries will find many ways to poke holes in their enforcement.

For example, how is the parent tracking two hours of weekday gaming, and four hours on weekends? Is there a stopwatch next to the console? Or is the parent in the house, being vigilant, for each and every one of those hours? Does this allotted time include watching streams and videos, or just the actual play? Who is checking that the child is in bed by 10 p.m. every night? (Is the parent home by then? Or already in bed?) What does this set of standards say about when the child needs to wake up? What does this say about expectations for their grades? These boundaries aimed for specificity but fell short. (Of course, no boundary plan is going to be completely kid-logic proof; they will always look for ways to creatively interpret your definitions.)

If you are insistent on capping the number of hours a day your child games, it will likely just become a nightmare of enforcement. Instead, I recommend shifting from this sort of very specific "only two hours a day" mindset to a more holistic approach. "Complete these items on your to-do list, and then you can play as much as you want until bedtime."

To extend the good behavior, you might add: "If you pull this off every day, you can stay up as late as you want on Friday or Saturday." The results are, believe it or not, pretty much the same thing. If they do everything they're supposed to do, all they might have time for is two hours of gaming anyway. And the added bonus of the weekend-of-freedom will be truly tempting to them—the idea of Mom or Dad not breathing down the teenager's neck on Friday can feel incredibly liberating.

Don't Forget Agency!

In chapter 3, I raised my concern that we parents are too often the ones who take care of things for our children. As in, take care of *ev-*

erything. When a big science project is due in the coming week, you probably continually remind your child about it, counting down the days until it is due, telling them what needs to be done, until they finally get started. But, as I said earlier, if this is how things go in your house, the only lesson they are learning is that they don't have to take responsibility, because you are always there to back them up.

It is therefore worth repeating: You need to give your child more agency—both to succeed and to fail. What happens if you just stop taking care of things for them? It can be shocking, dangerous, and somewhat damaging to the alliance—but perhaps necessary—to let them screw up every once in a while. You can still warn them a few days before an upcoming test with a comment that shows you're aware of but not taking on their responsibilities: "I see you've been gaming a lot, I hope you've been having fun! I assume that you're going to do well on this week's science test, as we agreed, and that you've got everything under control, as you've said. Good luck with your test in two days! If you don't get at least a B, remember that we talked about restricting your gaming time."

Let them know what's coming and remind them of the parameters they've agreed to. Then see what happens next.

If they forget to study and end up failing the test, talk to them again. They might come at you with a lot of resistance and no shortage of excuses: "My teacher doesn't like me, and that's why I failed." Stick with the communication tactics we have been working on, because guess what . . . "I told you so" never works.

Once again, the point of this whole program is to engender independence. You don't want to be nagging them constantly to cross the finish line—and you certainly don't want them to come to rely on your nagging to get things done. Give them some space to fail a little, so that they learn how important it is to rely on themselves to accomplish what needs to get done.

Dealing with Judgment Calls

You know what they say about the best-laid plans? They go awry. Because gaming technology is rapidly and constantly changing, boundary plans are destined to go awry, too, at least to some degree. Indeed, your boundary plan seemed pretty airtight when you developed it, but either your child will poke holes in it, or a technology will be developed that isn't technically covered in your plan. In these cases, your child will *believe they are complying*, but in your judgment, they're still failing. Your child will feel like the system is rigged against them—they can't possibly play by the rules if you keep changing the rules on them, they'll argue. Frankly, you'd feel the same way. After all, if you think you are following all the rules but getting punished anyway, why on earth would you respect the boundaries in the first place?

Let's say, for example, that both you and your child have agreed they can play two hours on weekdays and four hours on weekend days. When Friday rolls around, your child plays two hours and keeps at it. You say, "Time's up." But wait—is Friday a weekday or a weekend day? There are a thousand nuances like this that you won't think about ahead of time. This can create a breach—if you cut the gaming off at two hours on Friday, because you believe it is a school day, kids will find it unfair, because the boundaries were agreed upon but you two agreed on them with two different understandings.

Once again—this is a situation best handled at the weekly check-in! You can decide either way—against them or in their favor. But don't decide in the heat of the moment. Wait for the check-in and discuss what happened. For now, just make a note to discuss this scenario when you sit down to talk; after the check-in, you and your child can agree on what to do going forward.

Managing *Your* Emotions, Revisited

Few people make good decisions in a stressful moment.

This is why boundaries that are established in a moment of high emotions, or in response to a bad situation, are almost guaranteed to fail.

Let's say you've had a long day and from the moment you walked through the door, you've been taking a lot of sass from your cranky and boundary-frustrated child. You get fed up with their whining or their excuses (perhaps for not getting that homework done before dinner as you'd expected) or their refusal to shut the game off and go to bed. You asked at 10 p.m. You asked again at 10:30 p.m. Now it's 11:15 p.m., it's past your bedtime, you're exhausted, and you just lose it: "No more games for a week."

Notice that this new boundary is being set from a feeling of frustration. It's not well thought out. It has not taken into account the issues of scheduling, inconsistency, and enforcement we discussed earlier. How are you going to enforce it? Furthermore, at the end of a busy week, what is the lesson you are trying to teach?

Moreover, when you are reactive like this, you send the message to your child that you are an over-enforcer, which only bolsters their sense of your unfairness and rashness. Incidentally, it's worth noting that spontaneous or emotionally fueled *under-enforcement* (i.e., letting a boundary lapse because you're tired of fighting) does the same damage. In that instance, your child gets the message that your resolve can be worn down. Either way, when you discuss or negotiate boundaries when you are stressed or emotional, you lose because you weaken the alliance you've worked hard to establish with your child.

When boundaries are set as a result of mismanaged emotions, or are enforced unevenly, you are incentivizing behavior you don't want to incentivize. First, your child will learn that to keep their gaming access, it doesn't matter if they listen to their parents; they just need to figure out how to work around your explosions.

In the scenario above, your child will learn that they never actually need to listen to you at 10 p.m. But sometime between 11 p.m. and 11:30 p.m., you're likely to blow up, so they'll avoid listening to you until right before you're about to explode.

If this sort of scenario has happened before, and you haven't blown up, they've also learned that the 10 p.m. shutoff time is arbitrary. If they continue to game, as they have hundreds of times before, but this time you blow up and shut down their gaming for a week, it's pretty unfair. Your child has no way to see it coming. Neither of you is moving toward the goals you are aiming for, nor are you taking into account things that they value. They basically learn that their gaming access depends almost entirely on how moody their parents are.

Most concerning: If you have laid down a limit that you have no capacity to enforce, they learn that they don't even have to listen to it. They know you can't enforce it! So you are teaching your child to ignore your word. Same goes for if you say there is a punishment coming, but it never happens. There is no correlation between what you say and what you do.

That is why managing emotions is so critical. Never set a boundary when you're emotional. When boundaries are established through an understanding of shared values and open, careful discussion, you will be able to reinforce the lessons you actually want to sink in. Your words will be respected, your child will believe you to be a reasonable person, and they will come to understand that the reason you're restricting their gaming has to do with their goals and values, not your mood.

DO: Recognize that your emotions are a part of you, but they should not control you. If you are in a stressed or exhausted moment, hold off on discussing boundaries or changes with your child. Walk away for a minute and regroup. Then come back to the table with a clear head and a calm heart. The plan you will implement sets limits, as well as a time to talk, and a time to adjust. None of those three things need to be done when you are emotional.

Managing *Their* Emotions, Revisited

I know that your child's temper can be intimidating. In extreme cases, I've seen kids threaten their parents with the "nuclear option" of self-harm (or running away or hurting someone else) to get what they want. This is scary. You need to take their threats—especially of self-harm—seriously and get them help quickly if you're at all worried. But, most often, a child will say something drastic to get a rise out of you or to provoke the response—or de-escalation—they desire. If you are even dimly aware that you are being emotionally manipulated this way, *don't react.* You have to keep your mind in a practical space when setting and enforcing boundaries, because you both know how raw emotions are, and have been in your past, concerning this issue.

Tantrums are no easier to manage. Sometimes we just don't have the energy to deal with them; we prefer calm over conflict and will sacrifice a boundary in the name of peace and harmony. This is also completely reasonable—it's human nature—but if you are in this camp, you will want to lean especially hard into the alliance-building component of the program. Shouting should never have to be the only means of communication between you and your child. Keep working to prove to your kid that you're on the same team.

Remember that alliance building is not a one-time deal; it's a constant effort, and you'll never stop doing the work. (See chapters 5 and 6 for a refresher course on alliance-building strategies, and chapter 10 for more on tantrum taming and dealing with resistance.)

Let's recap the components of good and poor boundary setting.

POOR BOUNDARY DEFINITION
- Boundaries you are unable or unavailable to monitor.
- Boundaries with long time horizons without intermediate goals.
- Boundaries set when emotions are running high.
- Unilateral boundary setting—setting boundaries without buy-in from your child.

GOOD BOUNDARY SETTING
- Small, achievable goals that feel like wins.
- Boundaries that are established through calm discussion.
- Goals that your child helped set.
- Goals that you feel confident you and your child can achieve.

Developing a Boundary Plan—Part 2

STEP 1: ENGAGE YOUR CHILD.
- Engage your child in conversation.
- Ask open-ended questions.
  - Are they happy with the direction they are going in life?
  - Are they happy with how many games they play?
  - Share what your goals are. Ask them about their goals.

STEP 2: GIVE THEM A MENU OF OPTIONS.
- Recruit your child to figure out how they are going to make it happen.
- Give them a menu of options. You can pick the goal, but let your child weigh in on a menu of options concerning levers, metrics, and milestones.
- Channel your inner petulant monarch. You have a whim, and it is your subject's responsibility to make it happen. Dump it in their lap.
- Let them decide the levers.

STEP 3: DEVELOP A BOUNDARY PLAN WITH YOUR CHILD'S INPUT.
- They don't get to decide the boundary, but they get to control some of the levers.
- "What's important to you about gaming? Playing at a

particular time because your friends are on? Playing at particular hours?"

- Lay down the boundary you are going to institute.
  - Use the "dumping it in their lap" technique: "I need you to have a 3.0 GPA to continue playing games with your friends."
    - Take what's important to them and attach a condition to it.
    - You need to be relatively inflexible with this boundary.
    - Pick a target that you know your child can hopefully achieve (using the 25 percent rule).

STEP 4: FINALIZE THE BOUNDARY PLAN.

- Finalize all goals, levers, metrics, milestones.
- Double-check that you can reinforce everything.
- Confirm that you have your child's buy-in.

STEP 5: INSTITUTE THE PLAN, START WEEKLY CHECK-INS, AND COLLECT FEEDBACK.

- Notice that this step is not called "Enjoy Success." It is about acknowledging that an attempt has been made, and asking for an analysis of what worked and what didn't.
- Discuss where you agree and disagree about process and outcomes.
- If your plan is successful, *don't change your plan*.
  - This can be very confusing for your kid, because they will expect a reward for being successful.

However, you need to explain to your child that the success came as a result of this formula, and changing it will lead to a relapse.

- If your boundary plan fails, use differential diagnosis to approach the failure (see chapter 10). Ask yourself:
  - "Did I slip up because of my emotions?"
  - "Did I lack resources?"
  - "Did something unexpected happen?"
- Determine where and why you failed, then attempt to troubleshoot the problem spots the next time around.

Repeat.

CHAPTER 10

Enforcing Boundaries and Dealing with Resistance

We can build a wonderful alliance with our child, then establish the best boundary plan in the world. But no matter how many things you and your child have spent weeks discussing and, you think, coming to an agreement on, when the rubber hits the road, there is inevitably going to be pushback.

Where Resistance Comes From

Give yourself a break—pushback is to be expected. You are asking your child to change or even sometimes live without something that has great meaning to them and that might protect them from having to deal with uncomfortable real-life situations. Know that there are several strategies that can help you hold the line at every turn. We'll get into those here.

First let's try to understand where your child's resistance is coming from. I attribute part of my success as a psychiatrist, and my ability to help gamers, to something I learned while in India—the Vedic Model of the Mind, which elegantly explains what's going on when our kids fight us on changing their behavior. We'll start with the three most important concepts from the Vedic model: the *manas*, the *ahamkara*, and the *buddhi*.

The *manas* is our emotional mind (our most reactive part), the part that reacts and determines whether we like or dislike things. We don't actually control what we feel or what we want—if I eat a peanut butter and jelly sandwich, I don't decide whether I like it or not. It is just a reaction.

The *ahamkara* is our ego, or our identity, which the yogis think is entirely separate from our emotions or our thoughts. The *ahamkara* generates thoughts like *I am a doctor. I am a dad. I am a failure. I am a success.*

The *buddhi* is our intellect and the source of our analytical thinking and reasoning skills.

The purpose of the ego, our *ahamkara*, is to protect us from our negative emotions. Anytime someone feels a negative emotion, their ego will engage. I remember when I was in college, my friends would sometimes ask a girl out on a date. If the girl turned them down, they'd start to feel egotistical—"She doesn't deserve me" or "I wasn't that interested in her to begin with." When our mind experiences the negative emotion of a rejection, the ego arises to protect us. It behaves a little like a bouncer in a nightclub—its job is to keep the riffraff out, to protect you from the bad influences.

Now, the problem is that oftentimes the *ahamkara* will be incorrect. Any time the *ahamkara* is activated, it can conflict with our *buddhi*, or intellect. This is where the rationalizations or flawed reasoning come in. In the case of romantic rejection, if we aren't interested in the person, why did we ask them out in the first place? You may have found that when someone is thinking emotionally or egotistically, they believe they are logical, but their logic is flawed. And yet, even if you point out the flaws in their logic, their mind keeps twisting and turning, and coming up with new logic.

If there is a fight between your *ahamkara* and your *buddhi*, the *ahamkara* is stronger, and it will bully the *buddhi*, or intellect—"Hey, we're hurting, we need some kind of rationalization to make us feel better." And the *buddhi* complies. "Aye, Aye, Captain. Here's some selective reasoning to justify what you believe and to make us feel better."

If you're a parent, you may notice that if you talk to your child about gaming, you trigger this defensive crouch. No matter how logical you are, they don't see it your way and they argue continuously. That is because their intellect is being controlled by their ego, and there is no way that they're going to be wrong.

Incidentally, this is also why you can't argue with a narcissist. Narcissists are very insecure, and what triggers their narcissistic behavior is some kind of attack or any situation in which their insecurity comes to the surface. If someone makes them feel bad, they will attack that person, and their narcissism will kick in— they'll argue that they are better than whomever they are arguing with. You can't argue with them at this point, because all of their analytical reasoning is being controlled by their ego. No amount of logic will ever cause a narcissist to see your side of the story. When psychotherapists like me work with narcissists, we treat them with compassion and understanding and validation. Once the negative emotion has been removed, the bouncer doesn't need to protect us from anything; once the *ahamkara* becomes deactivated, you can reason with the person again. But it can never be an attack; otherwise you'll uncover their hidden negative emotion and reactivate their *ahamkara*.

What does this all mean when you're dealing with resistance from your gamer? You have to treat them a little like I would treat a narcissist in my practice. Let's say you tell them that they are ruining their life. The more correct you are, the stronger the resistance you will encounter.

If they really are ruining their life, they know it, but their mind is trying very hard to *ignore that*. The more on target you are, the stronger the negative emotion, which results in a dragon-fire-level response (even if they agree with you!). You will have activated their *ahamkara* and they'll immediately flip into denial mode. Then the negative emotions this accusation—and the ensuing argument—stir up will push them back into gaming. They'll likely come up with bizarre rationalizations to justify their gaming, and no matter how many logical arguments you make, they simply won't work.

Bottom line: Resistance is triggered at its root by negative emotion. When the *ahamkara* is active, it controls everything else, and your child will argue until they're blue in the face, denying that they have a problem. When I was in college, there was an overwhelming amount of evidence that I was about to flunk out of school—including letters from the dean saying exactly that. But somehow, I was still convinced that I would be fine—my *buddhi* was helpless against my *ahamkara*. It wasn't until I went to India that I understood this process of attack, denial, and resistance, and finally started to make some changes in my life.

How to Dismantle Denial

When your child is resisting you, whether it is them pushing back against a new system you're trying to implement or arguing against new house rules, almost all of us, as parents, tend to fall back on the old standby—using our authority to force obedience. When it comes to gaming—or any problem behavior—however, we need to empower our kids around the changes. We need to stay in control, but they need to feel some agency—some control over their lives—as well. Just as no one can force a person into sobriety, no parent can force their child into quitting gaming.

Remember: Resistance usually comes from negative emotions and triggers denial. Denial is a psychological defense mechanism. The more they feel they have to protect themselves from, the more they will try to deny. Like someone with a drinking problem who will stash their bottles and go to great lengths to hide their alcohol abuse from their loved ones, someone with problematic gaming habits—an addiction of sorts, too, as we've discussed—will deny that they have a problem. To them, losing access to their games also feels like an impending disaster, a devastating loss they will have trouble coping with. If you don't appreciate that psychological issue, you won't have their buy-in; they won't listen, and they'll resist.

A soft hand is your friend in this situation. A gentle approach of expressing understanding brings out a child's own admission that they have a problem. The harder you push them in a particular direction, the more likely it is that they will manifest some degree of denial.

We talked earlier about placing kids into two groups— pre-insight, when they aren't ready to admit they have a problem, and post-insight, where they are aware that there is an issue with their gaming. A pre-insight child is emotionally tranquil, and their capacity to understand the problem is different. With a pre-insight child, their *buddhi* does not understand that there is a problem—so they argue. With post-insight kids, their *buddhi* has been hijacked by their *ahamkara*—so they will still argue, but out of denial of the truth, rather than ignorance. Even though the response is the same—"I don't have a problem"—understanding the origin of the problem can help you as a parent move them forward.

In the case of pre-insight, ask them open-ended questions to increase their understanding. You can do this for post-insight kids as well, but remember that their defense mechanisms are rooted in their negative emotion. The way to decompress their hurtful emotions is to be emotionally validating, which is what reflective listening aims to do.

For a post-insight person, they know there's a problem. But even people who are post-insight will express some denial if you try to show them their problem by force. They'll say things like, "It's not as bad as you think." And they believe it themselves. That's just how the mind works. Their *buddhi* is developed, but they're in denial, because they are protecting against that negative emotion. There are certain things that get them to behave even more irrationally than usual. (I have coached many parents to pay attention to moments of really surprising irrationality. The more irrational your child becomes, the closer you are to something that hurts.)

Indeed, it's simply human nature that any time we're confronted with a negative thing, we try to sugarcoat it. We'll use any and all rationalizations to protect ourselves from an uncomfortable truth, because if we accept the problem as true, it makes us feel hopeless, which is a deeper psychological problem. So—as the logic goes— denial is protective. *As long as the problem isn't that bad, I can fix it.* But the worse the problem is, the harder it is to fix, and the more hopeless you become.

The key to disarming the ego and getting underneath denial is to decompress the emotion behind it. The more shame and guilt people have, the harder they deny that they have a problem. Getting through to a post-insight child requires disarming their *ahamkara*, through using open-ended questions and reflective listening. If you are open, curious, listening, and not attacking them, they no longer need protection, and their *ahamkara* will deactivate. When their bouncer takes the night off, you might actually be able to calmly discuss the problem without triggering their defense mechanisms.

Denial breaks down when a person hits rock-bottom—they have fallen so far that they have no choice but to acknowledge that they have a problem.

But I don't love the idea of waiting for kids to hit rock-bottom. At Healthy Gamer, our strategy is to intervene long before we get to that point, using authenticity and compassion to help someone recognize that they have a problem.

If you're noticing resistance from your child . . .

DO use the open-ended questions and reflective listening techniques we've been working on, then acknowledge their view before you try to share your own.

DON'T share your view as a direct counterpoint to theirs. Often, parents will say, "I understand what you're saying, BUT here's what I think." That can sound invalidating to your child.

DO try replacing *but* with *and*. For instance: "I can understand that your friends are very important to you, and you really enjoy playing video games, and that as a fifteen-year-old, it is your job to have fun. I totally get that. At the same time, it's also your job to be a student and learn. How do we reconcile those two things? How do we find some kind of balance?"

DON'T invalidate their feelings or deny them. It is the acknowledgment of someone's feelings that makes their need to deny weaken, and, over time, go away. In other words, if you validate and acknowledge how scared or uncomfortable your child feels with the idea of cutting back on their gaming time, they may start to admit that they have a problem with it.

Resistance Doesn't Equal Failure

In my psychiatry practice, I sometimes prescribe medication such as stimulants to my patients. And sometimes, my patients lose their medication, abuse the medication, or—I suspect—even sell it. In those situations, I explain that I'm sorry to hear it, but what they've lost is a controlled substance and cannot be re-prescribed until the first batch should have run out. They are never very happy to hear this.

Often, my young patients will push back and try to convince me that losing their medication isn't their fault; they always have a story and often find someone else to blame for the situation. I remain compassionate but I hold firm, despite their attempts to coerce me into re-prescribing it. "I'm not saying it is your fault," I say, "but I still can't prescribe more until next month."

More often than not, if I maintain my boundary and my resolve not to re-prescribe, my patients don't "lose" their meds again. Once they realize that there isn't a backup plan, they become a lot more careful and pay a lot more attention so as not to lose access to their medication.

If I handled this differently, perhaps by saying, *It's your fault—you should have kept better track of your medication*, we would inevitably get into a back-and-forth about whose fault this is, which is futile.

Here is what you need to remember: *Fault and boundaries are independent of each other.*

Instead of bickering over blame, you should acknowledge the failure, skip assigning blame (you can even concede that it isn't their fault), and yet confirm that you're still not moving the boundary. If my patient lost their medication because something bad happened to them—lost luggage, or a backpack rifled through at school—it is not my responsibility to correct the actions of the universe; I still can't re-prescribe their medication.

I know that this is a really hard position to take with your child, but it's vital. Just because it isn't their fault doesn't mean that you should compromise the boundaries you are trying to set. As soon as your child knows that you can be convinced to compromise the boundary, they also know you might do it again.

What if they have a really good reason, and you decide to compromise the boundary? Then what are you reinforcing? You're reinforcing that, for the right reason, the boundary can change. Then the game for your child becomes how to find the best reasons to convince you to violate the boundary again.

It's not that you can never compromise. Far from it—that is why I recommend that you make a weekly check-in. Hold the boundary now, then use your weekly check-in to have a discussion about it when emotions have cooled. That meeting is the time to decide whether to make an exception this one time, or to discuss changing the boundary itself.

Recognize that if you compromise a boundary once, chances are they will ask you to compromise it again. And, at the same time, if you're an inflexible jerk who doesn't listen to your child, you may damage the alliance. That's why you worked so hard to build an alliance—so the two of you can handle rough patches like this.

Let's say your child gets mono and misses a lot of school days and therefore doesn't meet their agreed-upon grade goals for the semester. How do you want to handle that? Do you want to give them a pass because their poor grades seem more like a product of their missed classes and not their gaming? If so, you need to pay attention to whether more excuses—and requests for passes—come down the line. If the goal keeps getting missed, point that out to them and talk it through. You want to ask open-ended questions, you want to reflectively listen, and then you want to be reasonable.

> You: Going forward, are you going to be right at the edge of missing an agreed-upon goal again? If it happens again, what do you expect me to do? Are you expecting that if you can come up with a good enough reason, the rules don't apply anymore?

The key point here is that once you've set reasonable boundaries and goals, you really shouldn't fold or dial back on them. The approach we teach at Healthy Gamer is what we call "rolling with resistance," or exploring the missed goal with the aim of understanding. At the same time, if you've been moving in the right direction with your child over weeks or months, offering a little latitude can go a long way. Once they start independently restraining themselves, that's when you can begin to look into the possibility of loosening boundaries.

Explore Their Resistance and Aim for Understanding

Your goal in exploring resistance is to learn something, not to prove something. Kids can tell the difference; they won't buy in to a conversation if you are using a question to make an argument. (The experts call that the "Socratic method," and it's best left in the realm of college professors, not to the parents of kids and teenagers.)

In general, people (who aren't being sarcastic or know-it-alls) ask questions because they *don't* already know the answer, right? In that sense, the question asker is ignorant—and that is the frame of mind you should have when you ask a question of your child. You are not the expert—you are ignorant. Being ignorant of something doesn't necessarily mean you are powerless, and your kid knows that. They know you still hold the power—and that it's in their best interest to enlighten you on what you claim not to know; holding out on you won't get them anywhere.

DON'T ask a question unless you are really prepared to listen to the answer and try to understand it.

DO honestly try to hear what your child is saying and understand them better.

TRY THIS: If, in a campaign to get you to allow them to game more at night, your child says, "That's my time to be with my friends," you can sympathize with that. You can say, "Wow, it must be really hard when 7 p.m. rolls around and I tell you that you cannot play anymore. It probably feels like you're losing your connection to your friends."

Your child will likely be confused by this turn of events—here you are sympathizing with them, clearly trying to understand them better. Keep rolling with this: "I can see that playing with your friends is really important for you. I am happy for you to do that as soon as your homework is done."

Make no mistake: I more than understand that when we're worried about our children, most of us talk a lot more than we listen. We tend to ask questions with the goal of proving a point. But what if we were to shift to asking questions with a goal of understanding instead?

Set aside time for regular discussions with your child that will not affect how much gaming they can engage in. Sometimes, you will need to separate boundary enforcement from conversation. If the boundary enforcement and conversation are part of the same discussion, your child will be disincentivized from even talking to you. Using the right language will help you establish a boundary but still encourage dialogue.

DO separate boundary enforcement from sympathetic conversation.

DON'T include gaming restrictions in your regular discussions.

TRY THIS: Ask open-ended questions, practice reflective listening, and offer emotional validation to help your child feel understood. Here's what that looks like in practice:

- Open-ended question: If you ask, "What about gaming is really important to you?" they might respond with, "I really enjoy playing with my friends. It's a lot of fun. We stay up very late."

- Reflective listening: You can say, "It sounds like playing with your friends is really important to you. Everyone in your friend group likes to play games after a long day of school, and you guys stay up super late playing."
- Emotional validation: You sympathize by saying, "That must be really hard. You probably felt like you were getting cut off from your friend group when I imposed restrictions on your gaming."
- "Let's talk about this on Thursday. If we can figure out some way to make sure you complete all the things you're supposed to, then we can be more flexible when it comes to spending time with your friends online."

Notice that you haven't budged an inch on letting your child join their friends online before the goal of homework completion has been met. But you *have* shown that you're listening to them and care about their feelings.

The goal of exploring resistance is to discover what your child values. Here are some more open-ended questions and statements to get you started, some of which you might have used back in the beginning, when you were just starting to build an alliance with your child:

- "Help me understand what makes playing video games so important to you."

- "If I set a limit on your gaming, what bothers you about that?"
- "What do you like so much about video games?"
- "If I set a limit of two hours of homework before the video game, help me understand what feels so unfair about that."

Their responses will lead to you an understanding of what the value of the game is to them. It will help you understand their perspective, and you can integrate that new knowledge into future boundary-setting conversations.

Part of changing the dynamic between you and your child when it comes to gaming involves dealing with resistance in a healthy way. Sometimes when you are faced with a lot of resistance from your child, your interaction just turns into a power struggle. You restrict, they react. It's an arms race—you make a spear, they build a shield, you find a sword, they come back wearing armor. At some point, someone throws a cannonball, and everything goes to hell.

An escalating arms race of discipline versus covert operations never ends well. If you use a "my way or the highway" strategy, your child will as well. "I'm a parent and I will do what I want." So will they.

This is about power—they are very good at playing this game, because that's the game you've been teaching them for a long time. Even if you win, everyone loses. Rolling with resistance is an excellent opportunity to finally model the right behavior to your child.

You Can't Tell Me What to Do!

A common conflict between older children and parents occurs when the child says, "I'm an adult. You can't tell me what to do!" Sometimes, this is somewhat true—an older child might have saved up to buy their own gaming system and their games, and they consider themselves too old to have to abide by your rules.

But you can dig into this more deeply. Ask them, "What constitutes being an adult? What are the responsibilities of an adult? Do you do those things? What's your understanding of why you don't?" Have an open-ended conversation about what it means to be an adult and what expectations of an adult they are, and are not, meeting.

Enforcing Boundaries in the Face of Resistance

Now that you understand why your child is resisting the boundaries you've put in place, and you've learned some techniques for rolling with their resistance, everything is going according to plan, right?

I say that facetiously because, of course, I know full well it's not always going to be that easy. You were already prepared for your child to push back, debate, argue, get sullen, and even throw tantrums. Some or all of that is going to happen—they are kids, after all. And they are having something they love and think they need withheld from them—it's human nature to get frustrated and angry.

Your child might tell you they feel like nothing they do is good enough for you. This statement will likely make you feel guilty. Your answer to a statement like this should not be driven by guilt, sadness, or any other negative emotion. To answer this question well and support your kid in that moment, you need to remove yourself from the equation. You can ask, "How long have you felt that way?" and say

"That must be really hard. What is it like to have a parent you feel you can never satisfy?" Simply listen to their answer and repeat back your understanding of what they said. (Reflective listening and emotional validation.)

But even as you do so, you must hold firm. Hopefully holding firm is going to be easier than you think, because the ask you're beginning with is very, very small. Remember: It's the tiniest hill you've started with—not the mountain. Indeed, this initial set of goals should be so simple that throwing a tantrum is actually more work for your child than complying with the task at hand would be.

That said, when you *are* dealing with pushback or a temper tantrum in response to enforcing a boundary, remember the techniques you've already been working on.

Use open-ended questions and reflective listening yet again:

"Can you help me understand why you're upset? Can you help me understand why this is so important to you?"

Then you reflect back: "I can see why you're so upset. It seems like you feel as if you're really missing out."

Use questions to get them to engage, then dump it in their lap:

"What's your understanding of why we set this boundary in the first place?"

"I understand that you want to play, but what do we do about your grades?"

This is the point at which they will fight back and probably start making promises both of you know they can't keep: "I'll play now, and I promise I'll do the work later."

You can't waver. This is when you stick with it and continue to enforce the boundary: "I can't always trust your promises—that's why we're here in the first place. You already promised to do the work. And you didn't follow through. That doesn't seem to be working."

If your child is resistant and does not see the problem, you could say, "I understand that you don't see a problem. I'm not trying to convince you that there is a problem. But my job as your parent is to set you up for success as an adult, and I don't see what you're doing as moving in that direction. I know that you don't understand it—I wish I could explain it better to you. But I have to ultimately do my job as your parent. I can't let you down just because you don't understand what I'm doing here."

Be very careful at this point, because kids will use your emotions and your love and deep care for them to convince you that you're hurting them. But if you cave, what you will be reinforcing is that *escalation on their part gets them what they want*. If escalation prompts you to cave on the boundary, you are training them to escalate. In other words, any appeasement you offer now will only lead to more temper tantrums. You'll have taken a couple of steps forward in this fight against problem gaming, only to be tossed backward, perhaps all the way back to the beginning again.

To state the obvious: It's important to stay firm. If your child is continuing to throw temper tantrums, don't tiptoe around them, and don't react to them. Instead, ask yourself some questions. How did we get here? If you truly built an alliance and learned to listen to your child, and you built a boundary plan that is aligned with their values, what went wrong? Did something change? Did the agreed-upon plan turn out to be overly harsh? Are you or your child starting to get emotional?

Then you need to start asking your child some questions, too, so you can solve this problem together.

First, reestablish the firm boundary: "I get that you miss out on your gaming, but the problem is that you haven't done your homework. Every time we talk about it, you list the reasons that you aren't getting good grades. I understand that sometimes life gets in the way, but, at the end of the day, the grades that you're getting are kind of unacceptable."

Keep having weekly check-ins, since these offer your child a chance to discuss changes to your plans. Remember that enforcement and modification shouldn't happen at the same time. These weekly conversations are not the time to levy consequences. Doing so will shut down this important weekly line of communication. Make this your mantra: Discuss together. Assess alone. Implement the change together.

Common Boundary Pitfalls

We learn new things by trying them, messing up, and trying again. So it goes with boundary enforcement. Never forget that you are dealing with a very modern problem, one that no generation before you has had to contend with. So, cut yourself a little slack. In the throes of your child's temper tantrums about the changes you are trying to make with them, remind yourself that your job is to be your child's parent, not their friend, just now. You are their guiding compass in all this. When in doubt, step back, take a breath, and ask yourself what it is they need from you *as their parent* in that moment.

Stick with What Works

One mistake I've seen a lot of parents make is that they change what got them where they are. Quite a few patients in my practice have depressive disorders. Sometimes, after six months on a medication, a patient will come back to me and say, "Hey, Dr. K, I feel so much better! I want to get off the meds now." I have to remind them that, even though they feel good right now, if they stop taking the meds that have helped them feel better, more often than not, they'll find themselves right back where they started.

If a particular strategy has been working, and you have made good progress, don't stop what you're doing now! That strategy is exactly the one you need to maintain.

In the throes of your child's temper tantrums about the changes you are trying to make with them, remind yourself that your job is to be your child's parent, not their friend, just now.

Stay Firm: Focus on Restraint, Not Restriction

The nature of your parental relationship will change as your child gets older and your guidance focuses on restraint, not restriction.

You're instilling the right values and the right discipline so *they* make the right choices. But know this: I have worked with a large population of eighteen- to twenty-four-year-olds through my Healthy Gamer platform, and they often say that they wished their parents had been stricter with them so that their gaming did not get out of control.

Don't set a boundary and enforce a boundary at the same time.

You can't create a new rule when someone is in violation of it already, plus punish them at the same time. Your child will most surely resent this. And, just as dangerously, this conflating of boundary setting and enforcement leads most parents to create extreme boundaries, ones that cannot be enforced over the long term.

Your love is appropriate and needed, but don't let it cloud your judgment.

Love for our children can actually be the number-one cause of a failed boundary. The logic goes like this: "Hmm, my child is asking so nicely, and they've been so good and sweet, and they did just get an A on the test. Let me ignore my own rules because I love them so much." Of course, we want to reward good behavior, and of course we all want to see our kids happy *today*—right now! But remember that love, in this case, looks like getting your child into the best position to thrive. Channel all your love into those weekly check-ins. But love includes setting and sticking to these boundaries.

If you're afraid, you will likely set too tight a boundary.

If you are afraid that your child is headed down a path that might "ruin their life," you may act or react very dramatically—for instance, setting a boundary that is, perhaps, disproportionate to your child's problem behavior. At least that's the way they'll see it. Indeed, this is incredibly confusing for the child, because when boundary setting is based on a drastic fear, it is actually divorced from the reality that they are seeing and experiencing. They, understandably, don't know whether what they are doing will "ruin their lives" or not. (That's what makes them kids and us parents.)

They will just react to what they see as your completely unhinged behavior. As a result, they will react very poorly to the boundaries that you set, because each party is starting from very different assumptions and very different worldviews.

Getting on the Same Page with Your Spouse

You and your spouse or co-parent are, of course, unique and will no doubt often have different interpretations of the same behavior. This may have even been something that attracted you to each other in the first place! But when it comes to raising a healthy gamer, you two need to present a united front: You need to agree that there is a problem, and you need to agree on the steps you'll take as a family to solve it. If you don't establish this common ground from the get-go, your child will find a way to divide and conquer!

You learned about the value of *open-ended questions* as a way to open up lines of communication with your child. Now use the same strategy with your co-parent.

Let's say you open with: "What do you think about our child's gaming?"

Perhaps this will be their response: "Oh, they'll grow out of it." Whatever they say, use reflective listening next to make sure you understand their perspective.

"Sounds like you think they will just grow out of it. Did I understand you correctly?"

Once you've understood their point of view, share your own concerns. You want to use opinion statements and acknowledge that this is just your opinion. If you try to make it a statement of truth, then it becomes an argument. A statement of opinion is more palatable; everyone is entitled to an opinion.

"I am concerned about his gaming."

Now ask your co-parent what they heard you say. This is going to be tricky because they are not going to repeat back what you said (unless they're also reading this book!). They are probably going to share their own opinion again.

In response, you can say, "I understand that that is your opinion, but did you understand what I was saying?" Sometimes, you will have to repeat this question. You can even tell your co-parent, "I'm not hearing you repeat back what I actually said. Can I try to share it again? I'd really like to make sure we're on the same page. I felt like I understood what you're trying to say. I don't feel like you're understanding what I'm trying to say."

Gently redirect them toward your opinions. Ask them to repeat what they heard you say and what your point is, irrespective of whether they agree or not. This is just about confirming the message that has been communicated, not about whether the message is right or wrong.

State clearly that while you acknowledge their point of view, you're highly concerned about the possibility of them being wrong.

"I understand what you're saying. There's absolutely a chance that our child will grow out of it. There's no doubt about that, but I have my opinion for a reason as well."

Keep in mind that you're not really looking to convince your co-parent that you're right and they're wrong. Try to get them to agree to what I call a "pilot program." This is where you can find some measure of alignment based on shared goals. Adapt what you learned in part two—but instead of trying to better understand your child, now you're trying to better understand your partner. You can ask, "Are you happy with our child's grades? Can we please try this approach and see if our child's grades go up?"

Dealing with Dueling Households

It's hard to set boundaries for your child when there are other people in their lives who aren't on board with the plan. This is hard enough when you are still partnered with this other parenting figure, but it's made harder when the person is an ex-spouse, someone you no longer live with or perhaps don't even communicate with.

Whether the issue is two dueling households or one divided one, the effect is that your child intuits that you disagree and therefore there may be leeway in the boundaries themselves. Kids can start playing favorites, which sets up the competing dynamic of good parent versus bad parent. Each parent wants their kid to like them a little bit more, of course, and, as a result, they can subconsciously be more indulgent to win their child's favor. When this happens, addiction can thrive. Boundary setting is very difficult unless all parenting figures are on the same page.

This isn't only about you and your spouse; aunts, uncles, and grandparents can sow confusion as well. All it takes is one parenting figure who ignores the rules to create a breeding ground for addiction to grow.

If you find yourself in the position of parenting a child whose other caregivers have differing opinions on gaming addiction, it helps to develop a common set of rules that all parenting figures can abide by. You and your co-parent might need to have some tough conversations. How are gifts given in the two households? How are limits set? What do rewards look like? What are the parameters of the boundaries set in each other's households, and are these boundaries enforceable? Do differing households have differing abilities to enforce agreed-upon boundaries?

You can do the same with the parents of your children's friends: Do we agree to enforce the group's agreed-upon restrictions in person in everyone's households? What about when they aren't together? Is there a shared time that we want to agree upon to have them all stop playing Fortnite at night? Try to come up with scenarios where you know you'll run into some trouble and pushback from your kids and agree on some solutions that might work for everyone. See below for more on talking with your child's friends' parents.

Talking with Grandparents or Other Caring Adults

Grandparents present yet another challenge for enforcing boundaries because they frequently believe that their role is specifically to "spoil their grandchildren." They remember what it was like to be a parent—too often having to be the "bad cop"—and now they get to focus on having fun and making their grandchildren happy.

The challenge when dealing with other caregivers like grandparents is that they may not recognize the consequences of their actions—they don't have to fight with their grandchild every night to go to bed on time. They just see the joy on their grandchild's face when they open a new game or console on their birthday.

I had one parent in our program who put this pretty succinctly—and rather rudely—but the sentiment was so accurate, I'll share it here: "The problem is that grandparents get to sh*t the bed and someone else has to clean it up." This parent vocalized their frustration at finding themselves having to "parent" a grandparent, too.

This means that as we try to do our job as parents and set limits on grandparents' gifts, we will often encounter lots of resistance from the other adults in the room. After all, they are just doing their "job," too—which is to love and spoil their grandchild. If you try to set limits on them, they may be affronted—"Are you trying to restrict my love?"

Grandparents or other well-meaning adults in this frame of mind will often dismiss your concerns: "It's just a phase. They'll grow out of it. You were like that, too, and you turned out fine." Arguing these points is a waste of time. Remember our discussion of the *ahamkara* in the last chapter? When we tell grandparents—whose job it is to love their grandkids—that their actions are *hurting* their loved ones, the *ahamkara* rises to protect them. If their intellect can deny that their actions are harmful, then they don't have to feel guilty! *You, you silly parent, you don't understand that being a loving grandparent isn't hurting anyone!* Their actions are *enriching* their child's life. Their mind slips into denial mode: *Everything is fine, I am not doing anything wrong, and I don't have to feel guilty or change my behavior.*

Try this kind of response instead: "I understand that spoiling our child feels like the right decision, but spoiling them with a cupcake or a toy is different from spoiling them with a video game."

It's important to be mindful that anyone who is a grandparent today did not grow up with the kinds of games now on the market. That is, they may not have any clear idea of what they are endorsing when they allow your child to game (in their house, or when they are watching your child). Start there and explain the ways in which gaming technology is addictive, and how concerned you are with your child's amount of play:

"There is a lot of evidence that these games and other technologies are very addictive, and I'm concerned that you don't really see the things that I'm seeing." (This might be because the grandparent doesn't live with the child.)

If appealing to a grandparent this way doesn't stop them from indulging your child's interest in gaming, you may have to set down a firm boundary. Remember: You are responsible for your child's health, and you get to decide if continued contact with someone who challenges that goal is in their best interest. Even if you are unwilling to threaten to cut the grandparent off entirely from seeing their grandchild, you might need to be very specific about the circumstances in which they can interact.

For example, perhaps you make a boundary that grandparent-grandchild interactions can only happen in a public place, away from technology, or only in your own home, during a non-gaming day, or that the only gifts you will accept in your household are non-tech-related ones. By laying these boundaries, you want the grandparent to understand that, at the end of the day, you are doing what you believe is best for your child. Remind them that they were in charge when you were a child, but you're the boss now!

Talking with Your Child's Friends' Parents

Having conversations with your child's friends' parents in an open-ended way can be incredibly helpful in presenting a unified front to the entire friend group. Try to set ground rules as a group—get everyone on a conference call, send a group text, or maybe even invite everyone to dinner. Ask them, "Hey, what do you think of your kid's gaming?" Listen to what they have to say. Use reflective listening. As people speak, maybe even take notes.

Afterward, present what you have heard from everyone and invite the group to come up with a plan of action. More often than not, you'll find your kid's friends' parents have many of the same concerns as you do, and they might have some good ideas about group boundaries you can all lay down.

Try to set the group's ground rules:

Do we agree to enforce the group's agreed-upon restrictions in person in everyone's households?

What about when they aren't together?

Is there a shared time that we want to agree upon to have them all stop playing Fortnite at night?

Navigating around Your Own Shortcomings

Now that we've talked about navigating pitfalls with other co-parents, caregivers, and your child's friends' parents, let's talk about you. Because if the issues you are facing don't actually originate with other people, the problem might be *you*. Indeed, I find that kids who are struggling with video games have parents who could almost always benefit from learning a few things.

The Timing of Boundary Reinforcement

The timing of boundary enforcement is important. The science of behavioral reinforcement tells us that it is vital to shorten the window between action and consequence. Pavlov didn't ring his bell and then wait four days to give his dogs the food. They would never have learned anything that way! The timing between the bell and the food determines the association. Likewise, video games are really good at instant gratification—they don't mail your reward to you within ten business days, you receive it in mere seconds and can play with it immediately. As a parent, you need to match the game's pacing.

If your child makes a mistake and you don't institute a consequence until days later, that's going to feel unfair because they might not even remember what they did wrong.

Same goes for positive reinforcement, not just negative. If they do something good, praise them as quickly as possible. Why? Because the time between an action and its consequence determines how strongly the brain reinforces or reduces the behavior.

Delayed gratification doesn't encourage behavioral change. The further away the reward is, the harder it is to get someone to do something. As parents, we want to take advantage of this principle. The closer the act is to the consequence (reward or punishment), the more your child will listen.

Of course, if one of the goals you and your child have set is for them to improve their grades, there is going to be a time lag between their efforts and their report card. How best to manage this delay vis-à-vis their access to gaming, which you've agreed to increase as their grades improve? Bake in milestones relating to the initial goal-setting/boundary-making conversation. Perhaps this means that you agree that incremental improvement on quiz or test grades will yield changes to the boundaries, but that the final semester grade is the "holy grail"—the proof (or lack thereof) that their gaming is getting under control.

As a general rule, the more warning kids have about restrictions or punishments, the lower the intensity of the temper tantrum that they are going to throw when you levy them. When your kids were toddlers, you likely learned that switching off the TV in a rush led to disaster—but offering a five-minute warning or setting a countdown timer worked to prepare your child for an unwanted outcome, and you avoided a dramatic meltdown.

Draw on that hard-earned knowledge when dealing with your gamer. Give your kids plenty of notice. They should know both the boundary and the consequences well in advance. It's okay to give them a reminder or two, but don't take responsibility for making it happen.

For example, if you've agreed that your child needs to get Bs this semester, you can say: "If you get one C, we are going to cut your gaming down by one day, during which time you will put in the work to get your grade back up. The more Cs you get, the more days of the week you are going to lose gaming."

The other advantage of a gradual reinforcement is that it focuses on *improvement* and not perfection—again, we are looking for movement in an overall positive direction, rather than an instant fix. Remember: It's easier to enforce a small boundary rather than a large, global boundary. When we institute boundaries in bite-sized chunks, the progress might be minimal, but it's measurable.

One more tip: Don't use "signs" of compliance as a substitute for compliance. Studying for three days in a row is not the same as acing a test. When you relax a restriction based on a *sign* of obedience, that teaches your child that they only have to pretend to do what they were supposed to (or do it for a finite amount of time), instead of actually achieving positive results.

Avoid Absolutes

Most parents will institute large-scale enforcement for brief periods of time. This usually starts with a catastrophic event, such as a huge argument or a bad report card. You run out of patience and come down hard on your child. You institute dramatic limits and draconian consequences—such as banning gaming altogether.

I hope it's obvious to you at this point that there are real down-sides to this approach, starting with your child's ramped-up anger and your increased stress; this kind of large-scale consequence can be incredibly damaging to the alliance you've been building. Fur-thermore, because this change—banning gaming—is so large, it is hard to enforce over time. As we've learned, when the boundary starts to deteriorate, your child learns that boundaries don't need to be respected because Mom and Dad are going to give in eventually.

When you turn to large-scale enforcement, have a conversation with your child about when the agreed-upon boundaries will get re-evaluated. As the parent, you *can* tell your child to stop gaming com-pletely, but oftentimes that kind of blanket lockdown does not lead to healthy relationships or open communication. When parents do this, they're generally letting their emotions run the show, usually after really frustrating moments with their kids. That is why I recom-mend reevaluating at regular intervals.

A word of encouragement: The most fighting regarding bound-aries will be at the beginning. And the longer the boundary has been loose, or nonexistent, the slower a child will be to adapt to it. If your child has been playing video games for a decade, it might be a five-year endeavor to wean them off the games.

Bottom line: It is important to learn to manage your expecta-tions. Accept slow progress. Trust the process. It is going to be a long path ahead, but, I can promise you, if you stick to the process, you will see progress.

Rewards Don't Have to Violate Boundaries!

Rewarding your child for good behavior shouldn't require you to violate your boundary when it comes to gaming. One way to do that is to give them rewards that don't have anything to do with games.

Some examples of non-gaming rewards are:

- Going to a sporting event.
- Getting them a dirt bike.
- Getting them merch, such as a jersey of their favorite sports (or Esports!) team.
- Letting them pick what the family is having for dinner or choosing the takeout place for the night.
- Access to a screen . . . to watch a movie.

Remember to Take Good Care of Yourself

Most situations in which I personally have been a less than stellar parent don't have all that much to do with my children; they have much more to do with my own inconsistency, fatigue, anger, and frustration. Parents are the first line of defense. Working on ourselves is one of the most effective ways to work on the kids we are trying to help. Your own behaviors as a parent directly affect what your child will do. Therefore, by gaining self-awareness, you can steer your gamer in the right direction.

When working with parent clients, I always point to extensive research showing that if a parent and a child have an anxiety diagnosis, and the parent is treated for anxiety, the child often gets better without their own specific treatment. Parents who see success with their child when it comes to gaming tend to be doing a lot of significant work on themselves as an intrinsic part of the process.

These parents are willing to explore their own weaknesses, adjust their own behavior, and boost their own emotional intelligence. If you think about it, your child's ability to manipulate you and push your buttons comes from your own emotional vulnerability. But they didn't make you emotionally vulnerable. They just were smart enough to figure out that weakness, then learned how to weaponize it against you.

If you aren't taking care of yourself, it's like driving with a flat tire. If you're not at your best, you will not be able to be there for your children in the best way you could be. The more you can focus on yourself, strengthen yourself, and get your own life in order, the more likely you are to be a strong, supportive parent for your child.

The cliché about putting on your own oxygen mask first, in a plane, before you try to help your seatmate (or child) applies here. Take care of yourself first, mentally and physically. Ideal parents are well-rested, so get enough rest, first and foremost. Then, be forgiving with yourself. Modern-day parenting is really, really hard. Self-compassion is very important.

Once your mind is in a tranquil and calm state, you are ready to be the best parent for your child.

PART FOUR

Common Challenges

Video game addiction can often be due to, or worsened by, an underlying mood disorder, undiagnosed ADHD, and even high-functioning autism. It can also be exacerbated by marijuana use. In fact, in my work with families, I estimate that one in three kids has something else going on.

This section will cover these issues, explaining why getting a professional evaluation for your child's behavior can be helpful (even if they end up not having any of these issues), how mental illness and gaming intersect, and how to adjust the core of my program to your child's specific needs.

CHAPTER 11

Confronting and Evaluating Mental Health Concerns

Sometimes, despite all your best efforts to implement the advice in these pages, and despite all your child's best efforts to work with you to turn things around, things don't click. When this describes your situation, you need to consider the idea that your child has a mental health issue that might be getting in the way.

Struggling parents—who feel like they have tried everything but nothing has worked—might think they're doing something wrong. In fact, you have probably been doing a lot of things right, and that is why you are starting to suspect that there is more going on with your child than an over-interest in video gaming.

That has put you in a bind—you were never taught to assess the clinical severity of potential mental health challenges in your child. And you also might feel that you're overreacting, or that you are in some way hurting their self-esteem by suggesting that they need to be evaluated in the first place. It's sort of a "which came first—the chicken or the egg" problem.

But you need to change the way you think about looking into mental health help for your child. Clinical help can mean *treatment,* but it is also about *thorough evaluation.* This is really important, because clinical evaluation to discover the *absence* of an illness is just as important as the diagnosis of an illness. Both affect your plan going forward.

I mentioned above that, in my own practice, about one in three kids has an underlying mental health problem that is coexisting with and likely exacerbating their video game problem. You need to know if this rough statistic holds for your child! Indeed, knowledge is power. A thorough diagnostic process can be incredibly satisfying, for you, of course, but, believe it or not, for your child as well. Oftentimes, parents know that something is wrong, but they see the symptom of the problem, not necessarily the root cause. Kids also might have a sense that something is amiss—and having a name to put to the feeling that there's something wrong can be hugely beneficial.

The Benefits of Getting an Evaluation

Consider the following scenario: Your child has trouble with impulsivity and emotional dysregulation—in other words, your child gets pissed every time you try to impose limits on gaming and throws a temper tantrum. It seems as if their brain is unable to put the brakes on negative emotions.

Impulsivity and emotional dysregulation are hallmarks of ADHD. If a child has ADHD, he or she is unable (at this moment)— or at least *less* able—to exert control over their amygdala with their frontal lobes. And if ADHD is the root issue, you'll need a proper diagnosis and professional help with emotional regulation strategies.

By using emotional regulation techniques to manage ADHD, your child will be able to reengage with life, and their gaming problem will start to improve. But this improvement cycle begins with an evaluation to help deal with the root issue.

It might also be that, when you get an evaluation, the therapist determines that your child *doesn't*, in fact, have ADHD or any other underlying issue. Now you know that all the acting out and temper tantrums aren't due to neurodiversity or impulsivity. What this tells you is that your child's issues are behavioral and environmental. Maybe they are throwing tantrums because one parent caves when they do, so they've learned that it is a successful strategy for getting what they want.

Both scenarios deserve our attention, our sympathy, and our care—but they also require different strategies entirely. In one case, we need patience and compassion—the child is suffering with ADHD, and we need to acknowledge that and adjust our approach accordingly. In the other case, we need firm boundaries and a No-BS attitude. Two completely different solutions for what looks like the same problem.

“

Clinical evaluation to discover the *absence* of an illness is just as important as the diagnosis of an illness. Both affect your plan going forward.

The threshold for seeking professional help shouldn't be whether your child badly needs treatment, but, instead, whether your child needs evaluation. So, simply start asking a different set of questions: Could mental health treatment *be helpful* in your situation? Could your child *benefit from* seeing a therapist or getting an evaluation by a psychiatrist?

And start thinking about a mental health evaluation the same way you would think about making sure your child gets an annual physical. Physicals are actually mandated by most school districts—without an updated vaccine record, your child can't attend public schools, and without an updated physical, your child can't participate in sports or other physical activities.

Resources for Finding Professional Help

If you need more help, there are excellent parent-peer support options available to you. Check out the Healthy Gamer website, where you'll find links to other resources—our parent Facebook group, our parent discussion forums, and various online communities.

Most of what we know from outcomes research is that the most important thing in a therapeutic relationship isn't a fancy degree, or years of experience, or similarities in ethnicity or religion. It's just fit. Both you and your child should feel comfortable with the therapist you are working with. Frequently people will try between one and three professionals before they find a good fit.

If you are seeking in-person professional support:

1. Speak to a medical professional and ask for a reference. Doctors are very good at connecting you to other doctors.
2. Talk to your child's school counselor. Tell them that you are worried that your child is having trouble with tech addiction and ask them if they can recommend local help.
3. Work your connections—ask family and friends if they know a good therapist.
4. Increasing numbers of patients are using the internet to find their care providers. Search on a map for "therapist" or "psychiatrist" to get started, and if the offices you call aren't taking on new patients, ask for other recommendations.
5. If you live in a country whose medical system is insurance based, contact your insurance provider for a list of approved and local therapists.

A Safe Place to Talk

Another important factor contributing to the decision to seek professional help is communication. A child behavior professional is trained in creating safe environments; if you're having trouble connecting with your child, or you feel that they aren't opening up to you, the safe space that a professional provides might be just what they need. By letting them share their more difficult and complicated thoughts and feelings with someone else, you will be giving them a great gift. Ceding the need to be the person they confide in signals to your child that you're there and ready, but that they can move at their own pace and in their own way. Bear in mind that, for many kids, the people they want to disappoint the least are their parents. It's not surprising that they might want to share their flaws with anyone *but* you.

I know this can be really hard—it's natural to want to be the one our kids confide in. Of course we want our kids to trust us and to feel that they can tell us anything. We spend our lives trying to make sure they know we love them unconditionally, and that we're always in their corner.

But getting fixated on creating the perfect environment to foster the level of openness you crave might not be the best use of your time. And time is of the essence—you want and need to get them help, fast.

My overwhelming experience as a physician is that for probably 99 percent of young patients, working with a therapist inevitably strengthens their relationship with their own parents. Before therapy, they didn't know what to say. How can they open up to you when they don't even have the right words to identify their feelings?

But once they work through some things with their therapist, they might have the ability to share their experiences with you. Just be patient and trust in the process. Trust that their work with a therapist will benefit them, then wait for them on the other side.

That's what parents do: You instill trust in your children that you will be there for them to support them in every way, on center stage or on the sidelines, until they can stand on their own two feet. If you do this right, someday, they will be ready to move out and live their own wonderful, independent lives, while knowing they can always come home to you.

How Serious Is Serious?

How do you know when calling in help from a professional is in order? Most parents ask me how to know "if things are serious." What does *serious* mean? Here are some examples of what I—and most parents—will consider serious:

- Impaired academic function made "visible" by their grades slipping dramatically or by a teacher or school administrator raising some alarm with you about your child's changing academic status.
- Changes in friendships or family relationships. If your child has a falling-out with someone who has been their friend for a long time, or if they suddenly start hanging out with a new crowd or individual, you should pay attention. Likewise if family relationships have gotten markedly tense.
- The absence of real-life friends.
- Extreme isolation, such as staying in their room all day, or not coming down for meals.
- Extreme dependence—difficulty getting out of bed, needing to be cleaned up after or cooked for.
- Tantrums that reach to the point of breaking things.
- Daily, or very frequent, arguments with you or other members of your family.

- Rebellious behavior like sneaking out at night or repeatedly breaking family rules.
- Self-harm, whether in the form of drug use, drinking, disordered eating, or cutting.
- Getting in physical fights at school or at home; harming others is problematic and serious behavior.
- Suicidal or homicidal thoughts or behavior—these warrant an emergency medical evaluation.

If your child has reached the point that any of the things on the above list are a more than infrequent occurrence, your suspicions are correct: Things are serious. It is time to seek professional help.

If they aren't at this point yet, it can be hard to figure out when exactly to reach out to mental health professionals. The bottom line, and the default I always encourage, is this: Take action sooner rather than later. Even if the visit is only for an evaluation, rather than for seeking necessary treatment, go see someone.

It never hurts to have more knowledge. With knowledge, you'll be better armed to help your child with their struggles.

CHAPTER 12

Challenge #1: Video Games and ADHD

The one thing that technology is consistently excellent at is fracturing our attention. Ever-shifting and constantly increasing technology speeds make it hard for us to be able to focus on one thing. Our attention span is withering because we're moving to shorter and shorter forms of content. A cultural reverence for movies morphed into a societal obsession with TV shows, but then there was a YouTube video, which got minimized into YouTube Shorts and TikToks. Books moved to blog posts, then finally just tweets. We don't ask that much of our minds anymore. A ninety-second Instagram Reel or aggregated headlines is about all we seem able to handle.

Whether directly attributable to technology or not, the rate of kids getting diagnosed with attention deficit hyperactivity disorder (ADHD) is growing year after year. And we also know that there is a clear comorbidity with kids diagnosed with ADHD also having problems with video game addiction.

What Is ADHD?

In recent years, there has been an explosion of research into understanding the brains of kids with ADHD, and the scientific community is just starting to understand how differently the ADHD brain is wired.

We now know that there are three things that are different about the brain of a child with ADHD.

1. Attention span
2. Impulse control
3. Emotional regulation

Attention

As the acronym suggests, ADHD is primarily characterized by a disruption of attention.

An average attention span has a couple of features—first, we can focus on something we direct our mind to, and if we want to shift our focus, we can direct it somewhere else. If your non-ADHD child is reading a book, and you call them to the table for lunch, they can process that you are talking to them, and they can usually put down the book and walk over to the table to eat.

Children with ADHD have trouble with this function. Because they are focused on the book, they can't also really hear what you're saying or focus on what you're asking them to do. When you look at studies of parents with ADHD kids, they yell a lot more than other parents. It's not because they're more cruel; it's because they've learned that a higher volume is required to break through the child's attentional wall.

In addition to you having trouble breaking into your child's attention, your child's attention can wander without their control. They have difficulty focusing on a particular thing. You might have to remind them of something repeatedly. You tell them once, they forget; you tell them again, they forget a second time; and so on. Confoundingly, this struggle for attention control goes both ways—either by shifting their focus away from something they want to focus on, or keeping it on something they don't want to focus on. This second scenario is best described as "overly sustained attention." In other words, when someone with ADHD gets stuck on something, that have a huge amount of trouble getting unstuck.

Impulse Control

We know that the human brain integrates input from what we see, what we hear, and what we feel. Do we feel hungry? Do we feel thirsty? We also get input from our mind—am I curious about this thing, or am I distracted by that thing?

In a neurotypical brain, we integrate this input, then we decide whether to act on an impulse or restrain the impulse. We might feel like going to the bathroom, or breaking into song during a work meeting, but we are able to delay doing so right then and there.

But all of this circuitry is wired differently in a person with ADHD. For kids with ADHD, we find that, first, sensory input creates a lot more impulses, and second, their ability to rein in those impulses is weaker.

What does this look like if you're a parent? You might have your child sit down to do their homework, but any kind of noise, even a bird flying outside the window, can distract them. Then, the moment they get distracted, they get up and wander off; they are unable to control that impulse.

Emotional Regulation

A lot of kids with ADHD appear extremely willful, tenacious, and prone to fixation. A child with ADHD can behave like a pit bull with something clamped in its jaws. They won't listen; they persist, for instance, in gaming; and, if you try to take the game away from them, they'll throw the biggest temper tantrum in the world. In an instance like this, parents often note that the reaction is far out of line with rational behavior.

When the ADHD goes undiagnosed, parents tend to just think their kid is extremely stubborn. But extreme stubbornness is a sign of emotional dysregulation—and ADHD.

Several studies, in which researchers scanned the brains of kids with ADHD, have found that negative emotions hit them faster and stay with them longer than in a neurotypical brain. Practically speaking, this means that children with ADHD will feel angry, frustrated, or sad faster than a neurotypical child. Furthermore, once these emotions arise, they persist in the brain for longer periods of time.

The Struggle Is Real

Kids with ADHD already struggle in life in countless ways. From preschool onward, they have usually had trouble fitting into the box that society—parents, playgroups, preschools, and then the odyssey of K–12 school—wants to put them in. Bottom line: Being a kid is not easy these days, and it's far harder when you've got ADHD.

The result is often academic underachievement, because the smallest distractions—again, that bird outside the classroom window—make their mind (or their whole body!) wander. Other times, the distraction could be as simple as another child giggling on the other side of the room—your child stops paying attention to the teacher and instead only pays attention to the kid who is laughing. It's a pretty straight line from not paying attention in class to doing poorly in school. And, unfortunately, a child who distracts the class or needs extra attention and monitoring by a teacher doesn't always get the compassion they so desperately need from that teacher; instead, the teacher just gets frustrated with them and might even lash out at them, compounding the problem.

It's not just teachers who treat them differently. Many kids with ADHD struggle with their peers, too. Let's say I'm six, I'm playing with my friends, and we're all taking turns doing something. But if I can't restrain my impulses, I don't wait for my turn—I'm going to jump ahead in line. And if I jump ahead, how are the other kids going to respond? Not well. Most kids can forgive the occasional going out of order, but if one child does this repeatedly, they are more likely to be unpopular, and even actively shunned.

We know that for children with ADHD, succeeding in life is harder, and maintaining relationships is harder. The wild thing about

ADHD, though, is that these kids oftentimes have an average or even above average IQ, which is, paradoxically, even more devastating.

The child with ADHD knows that something is wrong. Even a seven-year-old can look around the playground and see that everyone else has friends and wonder why they don't have friends. "My classmates always get invited to other people's birthday parties, but no one invites me." Or "I feel like I'm just as smart as these other kids, but they're getting As and I'm getting Cs."

This type of awareness of the situation helps us understand why a staggering 70 percent of kids who have ADHD will grow up to have depression. Children take all of these differences and internalize them, because that seven-year-old doesn't understand that their brain is wired differently. All they see is that people don't like them, and that they are failing.

A child with ADHD has very few outlets in which they feel they are thriving. So the adaptations they choose are often unhealthy: avoidance, suppression, and procrastination. Sometimes they turn to drugs (often marijuana; see chapter 15) or other substances and—of course—to technology.

Video Games Are a Custom-Built ADHD "Solution"

Games suit the ADHD brain perfectly: They're built to be fast-paced, stimulating, and engaging. A video game has lots of bright colors and loud noises, it is adrenaline-charged, and it holds their attention.

Video games allow the player to focus, progress, achieve, compete, fit in, and win—all the things they struggle with in everyday life. When video games enter the picture, the playing field levels out.

Think for a second about a time when you have been hyper-focused, when you've been in the zone—when both your body and mind were focused on one important thing, and you were in a flow state. Maybe you're writing or drawing or running or playing the piano, and you're just on—think how good it feels to be really dialed in, and to have your brain functioning exactly as it's supposed to.

Now think about this: ADHD kids only get that feeling from video games. The video game provides exactly the right level and kind of sensory stimuli that children with ADHD need to dial in and be able to focus.

Video games appeal not only to their specific attention span, but also to their impulsivity. A child with ADHD can often sit down and play a video game for hours at a time—all of their impulses simply go by the wayside.

Last, video games actively help people suppress their emotions, so they help an ADHD child with their emotional regulation. With the click of a button, a person with ADHD can engage their brain with something that will help them calm down. This is a huge relief to the ADHD brain.

Unfortunately, while all those bright lights, interesting sounds, and very engaging gameplay feel good to the ADHD brain, they can actually *compound* ADHD. Remember: These games make it easy to focus so your child doesn't have to train himself to pay attention to the video game; the video game provides so much sensory stimulus that the focus becomes automatic. But the more they outsource their focusing ability to the video game, the worse their attention span will get. The more video games they play, the worse their focus gets, which makes it that much harder to succeed in the real world. The harder it is to succeed in the real world, the more they retreat back into video gaming. So this becomes a vicious cycle.

If ADHD isn't on your radar, put it on your radar and consider getting a clinical evaluation. If an evaluation determines that your child does have ADHD, you will have to address the ADHD first—by getting your child accommodations in school and/or treatment. Until you address the ADHD diagnosis, their behavior when it comes to video gaming will be hard to control. Why? Because even as video games effectively atrophy your child's focus and impulse control, gaming feels *good* to their brain. So, if your child only has one opportunity to be focused and successful, it's going to be hard to take that opportunity away.

This is one of those situations where, unfortunately, there isn't a simple step-by-step solution. But after getting an evaluation and diagnosis, we know that psychotherapy—where your child can talk about their frustrations and work on strategies for mediating them—and medication can certainly help.

At-Home Strategies

Once you have professional help in place, there are things you can do at home, too.

Executive functioning refers to our ability and capacity to plan ahead in order to meet goals. As we've discussed, kids with ADHD struggle to follow directions and stay focused, so they tend to have trouble following multistep plans without getting distracted or interrupted. This is a real struggle when it comes to things like managing increasing responsibilities in school as they get older.

The more that you can help your child organize and focus in the rest of their life, the more success you'll have at reducing their intense interest in gaming. Working with your kid on specific executive functioning skills, like helping them figure out how to get themselves organized for the school day the night before and the morning of, may be really useful as well.

You can also support them in their efforts to better keep track of and manage their workload—planners and journals are helpful, as are checklists and very specific daily schedules. It is also important to try to teach them how to study, within the parameters of their skill set. No matter where they are on the ADHD spectrum, you and your child should be able to find their academic strengths and weaknesses and work together to capitalize on their strong points.

You can and should also talk to your child about the connection between the way their brain is wired and their video gaming.

Because ADHD tends to have less of a stigma associated with it than other mental health conditions, your open-ended questions can sometimes be quite direct:

> *What do you know about ADHD? Have you ever been worried that you might have it?*

If your child doesn't know much about the diagnosis, you can work around the edges a little:

> *Are there tasks related to school and stuff that seem to be easy for other people, but feel like they're hard for you? Can you tell me a little bit about that?*

Even if the stigma isn't as high, ADHD still carries an immense amount of shame with it, because it is extremely hard for a kid to see other people casually accomplishing things that their brain simply cannot do. Address that shame and frustration if you see it:

> *Do you sometimes get frustrated by your inability to do certain things that should feel easy?*

> *Hey, these struggles sound really tough. And they're not your fault at all—some people's brains are just wired differently than others. What do you think about seeing someone and potentially getting evaluated so we can come up with some new solutions?*

It is also important to carefully address the *consequences* of ADHD. You can use open-ended questions to delve into how your child is absorbing these outcomes of their condition. Ask them what their lives look like as a result of their ADHD:

> *What are your social relationships like?*

> *Do you get bullied?*

> *Do you always feel the need to be the class clown?*

> *How is your academic performance? How do you feel about that?*

Ultimately, remember that the key to overcoming gaming addiction is to allow your child's psychological needs to be met by the real world, instead of the video game. That is an especially difficult battle with ADHD. A child with ADHD has even more needs being met by the gaming than neurotypical gamers, and they probably have even more discomforts that the games are helping them avoid. But this is not an insurmountable challenge!

Cool That Thought

One emotional regulation strategy I like to teach my patients is to take advantage of the "mammalian diving reflex." I call this "ice-diving."

Don't worry—there are no swimming pools of ice involved, nor do you have to live in the Arctic. Ice-diving is a meditation/grounding technique you can practice at home. Often, when someone is emotionally dysregulated—they are crying or angry or having a temper tantrum—this is a result of the activation of their sympathetic nervous system. Remember that this is triggered by our amygdala, the source of that fight-or-flight response. Adrenaline and cortisol rush into our bodies, our heart is pumping fast, and our thinking patterns have lost any nuance—everything is black or white.

When we are in this state, we need to shut off that adrenaline because it is changing our thought patterns. The mammalian diving reflex does the trick. When mammals fall into cold water, their breathing and their heart rate immediately slow down. The brain also shuts off adrenaline production to force the body to relax and have a better chance of surviving.

You've likely experienced this yourself if you've gone swimming in a cold lake or pool. If you enter slowly, each step feels painful, right? But when you jump right in, after the initial shock, immediately your body numbs everything, and you're okay. Therapists, especially those who work with kids with ADHD, teach their patients to take advantage of this natural physiological hack in the brain. The mammalian diving reflex can be kick-started by immersing your face in cold water. Take a sink or a bucket, dump some ice in it, fill it with water, and quickly immerse your face.

Obviously, your child won't be able to plunge their head into an ice bath at school, but with some planning ahead (and the cooperation of their school), perhaps they could have access to ice cubes. Holding one in their hand (and switching hands when the near-painful numbness starts to set in) will trigger the same response, just in a smaller way, and will help focus their mind.

CHAPTER 13

Challenge #2: Video Games and Autism Spectrum Disorders

For many reasons, ranging from awareness of it to better diagnostics for identifying it, autism spectrum disorder (ASD) diagnoses have increased by a factor of five in the last fifteen years. There is also a high comorbidity between ASD and video game addiction.

As the word *spectrum* indicates, autism can range from extremely mild cases to extremely severe ones, and there may be a lot of diversity of experience. In cases of severe autism—where a child is not hitting developmental milestones for speech or social interactions—their case may be diagnosed when they are quite young. On the other end of the spectrum, there is high-functioning autism, where a person is very capable and can communicate very well. Indeed, people with high-functioning autism can appear neurotypical, especially if they also have a high IQ. Furthermore, many people develop compensatory mechanisms—both parents and kids—to address autism, which help conceal the condition from others and make a definitive diagnosis difficult.

That said, our diagnostic tools are getting better and better, as are our support and treatment options. If your child seems to have some of the traits listed below, consider getting them evaluated for ASD:

- Social difficulties
- Repetitive or continuous behavior, known in medical terms as "perseveration"
- Impulsivity
- Lack of empathy for others
- Behavioral problems and tantrums
- Inability to see your point of view

Without an autism diagnosis, you may not be able to figure out how to effectively set boundaries, as outlined in part three. If your child has autism, there might be important variables missing from the standard equation we've laid out for you—such as the ability to communicate or answer open-ended questions, and the ability to accept other points of view from their own as valid. This gap in understanding between a child with autism and their parent(s) makes things very frustrating for both parties.

How Video Games Complicate the Autism Picture

One of the things that some people with autism struggle with is their empathy circuitry. The way the autistic brain has been wired gives them trouble reading between the lines. Explicit information—that which is stated outright—they can handle. But many people on the autism spectrum have difficulty with implicit information (like social cues), so they can find the world pretty confusing. Unfortunately, the rules of how to function in the world are not always clearly explained. They might ask a significant other: "Are you upset that I forgot your birthday?" Their partner might answer, "No, I'm not upset. It's fine. I know you're busy." But they *are* upset! A neurotypical person will understand that they're upset; someone on the autistic spectrum may not.

That is why gaming is so attractive to someone with autism—the engineered world makes sense, because everything is explained to you, and the boundaries, rules, and scoring system are explicit, clear, and unchanging.

It's not just that games feel very understandable to someone with autism. Kids with ASD gravitate to games for many of the same reasons as those with ADHD do—gaming meets many of their social needs. Children with autism often have trouble relating to their peer group in face-to-face interactions, so their social difficulties might already be quite firmly baked in before they even start video gaming. But what might be a baseline avoidance of most social situations will only be exacerbated by a burgeoning preference for online-only socializing. After all, gaming offers some people with autism a new—and far more comfortable—social outlet because everyone is on a level playing field. There are no facial expressions or tones from others to decode, nor body language to exhibit themselves.

Many, if not most, people with autism appreciate repetitive behaviors and highly structured environments. They thrive on routine. Video games fit the bill, making it easy for a child to hyperfocus on accomplishing one task in an online world, not to mention allowing them to disappear almost entirely into that world.

Gaming can also offer a lot of consistency, which is very appealing to some people with autism. They may not play games like Fortnite, which are more unpredictable, but games known as "massively multiplayer online role-playing games" (MMORPGs), which have a lot of repetitive tasks that you need to do in a specific and predictable order, are highly appealing.

What to Do Next?

To help a child with autism taper off their video game use, you still need to follow the strategies for defining and setting boundaries that we discussed in part three. Generally speaking, however, you need to be much more concrete in doing so. For children on the autism spectrum, abstract thought may be a bit harder, so specific goals can be helpful; you have to be very explicit.

For example, open-ended questions can be extremely difficult for someone with autism spectrum disorder to respond to. Instead, they tend to have very concrete thinking, so you may need to use close-ended (i.e., yes or no) questions.

> *Are you concerned that your autism is part of the reason you are playing so many video games?*

> *Are you anxious when you are with other people?*

> *Do you play video games because you feel more comfortable in that world than with other people in real life?*

Setting expectations concerning boundary enforcement is also very important, but give your child on the autism spectrum an opportunity to adjust at each stage of the process. Establishing and tightening boundaries can be very disruptive and can lead to a lot of emotional volatility from kids on the autism spectrum. Be as gentle with your child as possible and take everything one step at a time.

Changing boundaries with kids on the autism spectrum is harder than with a neurotypical child. It's not about the size of the change, but the fact that the boundary is changing at all. The good news is that after you establish a routine, you'll have less of an uphill battle, because children with ASD often prefer to stick with routines once they have gotten used to them.

Last, keep in mind that in-bedroom access to gaming increases game usage by 50 percent. It is therefore that much more important for you to get the console out of your child's room if they are on the autism spectrum.

Likewise, you may want to limit access to the MMORPGs I mentioned earlier, because some studies have found that these role-playing games correlate with what we psychiatrists call "oppositional behavior." Oppositional behavior—constant defiance, excessive anger, or excessive irritability—may already be an issue for a child on the autism spectrum, so you don't want to add to the problem by allowing them to immerse themselves in a game that could bolster it.

Please Get Help

If you have a child who is prone to oppositional behavior, whether it is a result of ADHD, ASD, or any other complicating factors, the most important thing I can tell you is this: Get therapy!

Standard parenting techniques—and the basic assumptions around how to parent—may not work for kids with oppositional behavior, and they might not work for kids with ASD. Usually, parents have adapted to some of this over their many years of parenting, but, even so, getting clinical help is very important. And not just for your child—get support for yourself!

Sometimes, when a child is on the spectrum, neither the child nor the parents realize it. That is because the parents implement adaptations in their routines and make adjustments to their parenting style to help their child succeed in the world. Eventually, they figure out ways to make a square peg fit into a round hole.

But even if you're making do, a really good clinician is very important. It is the role of the clinician to tell you what your child can handle, and what they can't handle.

There are a lot of times where someone with autism can actually do something, but they use their illness to get a pass. There is a fine line between allowances we make for people with this challenge and the level of accountability or responsibility we demand of them. Because our kids are maturing and developing, and their capacity is in flux, it can be difficult to know how much is too much to ask. It can be very helpful to work with a professional who may be able to guide you in knowing if you're hitting the sweet spot.

CHAPTER 14

Challenge #3: Video Games and Depression or Anxiety

M ost adolescents are, at some point or quite often, a little bit moody. Sometimes they'll talk back. Sometimes they'll isolate themselves. Sometimes they'll have difficulty getting out of bed. Given that these are hallmarks of *just being a teenager*, it can be really confusing to try to figure out whether this behavior is a normal part of a teenager's life or if this reflects a clinical illness.

It's not just teenage behavior that can be worrisome. Older children have setbacks in life—perhaps your child graduated from college and they've had difficulty finding a job, which has made them feel sad about themselves and damaged their self-esteem. Maybe they have trouble getting out of bed in the morning. As a parent, you're left wondering, Okay, how much of this is normal life, and when does it rise to the level of depression?

Clinical depression can be very confusing, especially if you— the parent—don't see anything specific or know of an event that precipitated your child's general sadness or negativity. You might be especially confused if you haven't grown up witnessing or experiencing depression in your family or among close friends. When you grow up without depression, the only time you are sad is when something is wrong. But understand this: The whole reason that depression is a clinical illness is that you can feel bad even though *nothing is wrong*.

Of course, everyone has circumstances that make them sad. But an inability to bounce back after something sad happens may require therapeutic intervention. Being sad for a month or two after a breakup? Probably not an issue. But when the duration exceeds that time—or doesn't seem to be easing up in the least—I take note.

For purposes of understanding if your gamer is also depressed, we need to focus on the roots of the problem, rather than the symptoms: anhedonia, or the inability to experience pleasure, and a negative self-attitude.

Anhedonia

Normally, life has a lot to offer that excites us—fun events, delicious food, exciting plans. Perhaps your child usually looks forward to going to a party and seeing their friends on the weekend. Or maybe they love to go to the movies. Or they really get a kick out of getting ready for Christmas, giving and receiving gifts, and spending time relaxing with family.

When someone is clinically depressed, their ability to derive pleasure from activities that they normally enjoy is impaired. This means that life feels bland to them, and they have very little motivation to get out and do the things that used to bring them joy. Even eating can feel like a chore. Spending time with their family or going shopping or going to the movies or going to a party feels difficult because not only is the anticipation gone, so is the delight. When a depressed person stops enjoying life, they have to push themselves to engage with it, which, in turn, leads to exhaustion.

You know your kid—you know what makes them happy. When that thing or those activities stop working, that's anhedonia. Even cranky, moody teenagers still like doing things they love. Anhedonia is different.

Negative Self-Attitude

On a good day, we tend to think good things about ourselves—*I'm brilliant* or *I did that thing well.* On a different day, we might be a whole lot less charitable with ourselves: *I'm an idiot!* Over the course of a month in your life, all those statements are completely commonplace thoughts for a human brain.

But remaining in a persistent state of self-criticism is what clinicians call "negative self-attitude." Endless cycles of shame, guilt, hopelessness—the persistence and tenacity of those thoughts over time, all day, every day—are not normal at all. When someone has a persistent negative self-attitude—in which they think they have very little hope for the future—suicidal thinking can emerge.

When I work with patients who are clinically depressed, I often hear them express a negative attitude about themselves. They'll say things like, *My family would be better off without me. I'm sort of a waste of space. I don't bring joy to anyone in this world. People would be happier if they never saw me again.* This kind of negative attitude about themselves may be accompanied by a lot of emotions, such as sadness and guilt. This can also look like extreme frustration or anger with oneself. While sadness, self-esteem problems, even occasional suicidal ideation during intensive periods of stress can actually be a normal part of life, this kind of persistent negative self-attitude is specific to depression.

Gaming and Depression

How do video games intersect with the clinical picture of depression? Remember that when your child suffers from anhedonia, they have difficulty deriving pleasure from things that they normally enjoy. But what if there was an activity out there that was specifically designed to release dopamine into the brain, something designed to cause you to feel enjoyment, even if it's artificial enjoyment? Look no further than video games. Video games are all about that dopaminergic release within the brain.

Now let's think about negative self-attitude. If your child is depressed, they have all these negative feelings. Now imagine that there was some kind of activity that suppressed negative emotions. Do you think that would be appealing to someone who is clinically depressed? Absolutely. And that's exactly what video games do.

There are more subtle aspects at play here, too, not just at the neuroscientific level. If your child is depressed, we know that they have a negative self-attitude, and they feel like they're a waste of space in the real world. But in the virtual world, they have this virtual identity that other people respect and like. When they play a video game, they are never some bit player; they're always the central character. They're always the hero, and often the winner. They are always someone special. For a person who is struggling with depression, a virtual environment in which they can feel amazing can be incredibly addictive.

What Are You Noticing?

Your child may not seem sad or be crying all the time, but if you're paying attention, you'll likely notice subtle changes nonetheless. Anxiety (which we'll discuss specifically in the next chapter) can often look like depression, and garden-variety anger and frustration can, too. But is your child withdrawing or having difficulty engaging in the activities they used to engage in?

Perhaps you used to feel confident that, on a bad day, you were pretty good at making your child smile. If they were having a rough week, you used to know what to do about it. But now, a lot of the techniques that you used to deploy as a parent don't seem to be working. When we're talking about a clinical illness, that's exactly what happens.

When that anhedonic circuitry becomes active, and children aren't able to enjoy what they normally enjoy, you might see your child intensely retreat into video games. Your parental instinct is telling you that something is wrong because gaming is isolating them from others. They're irritable, they just go upstairs, they're not hanging out with their friends.

Your understandable instinct may be to quickly course-correct: You try to take away the video games and get them back to seeing their friends or back out on the mountain bike trail where they used to be so happy. But if your child is anhedonic, your well-meaning strategy will backfire because the reason they're playing the video game is because the things they used to enjoy don't trigger the same response for them anymore. Those friends or those mountain trails just don't bring them enjoyment.

This is equally frustrating for both parent and child. They do not enjoy doing this activity, but you are forcing them to do it, and it's just not doing anything for them. This is isolating for the kid, and they will react with anger and frustration. Now your child really feels that you don't understand them. This will be even further isolating, and their reaction is likely to be additional anger and frustration, and now it will be directed at you.

Bottom line: When they are in a clinical depressive episode, the rules of the game have totally changed.

Get Talking, Not Solving

As I've said from the start, the first thing you need to do is *talk* to your child. Sit down with them and give them space to open up. Depression is such a common topic of discussion among teenagers these days, especially in online communities, that they might be ready and willing to discuss it with you.

Do you and your friends ever talk about depression?

Here are some of the things that I'm noticing. Can you help me understand a little bit about what you're experiencing?

Have you ever been concerned that maybe depression could be affecting you?

It helps to use a lot of caveats—using words like *maybe* will make it easier for your child to ease into this conversation, rather than feel they are being accused of something. As usual, use open-ended questions and reflective listening, and don't try to judge or fix what they have to say. This is hard to do because of your own emotions. The hardest time to do reflective listening is when your child is suffering. If your child opens up enough to share suicidal thoughts with you, it will be very, very hard for you not to panic. (Remember the amygdala? Now yours is super-active—of course it is!—because your child's life is in danger.) Your job as a parent is to let your child talk—and for you to listen. Once the two of you have talked, though, it is important in the case of suicidality to seek immediate professional help.

They might respond to some of these questions with, "Yeah, maybe," to which you can listen and acknowledge their answer, then perhaps nudge them to expand.

Can you help me understand that?

Reflective listening is particularly important for conversations about depression. What this *doesn't* look like is all too common:

YOUR CHILD: "It feels like no one likes me."
YOU: "Well, of course everyone likes you. I love you. You're the most beautiful child in the world, and you're amazing!"

This might feel like just the right thing to say—you do love your child, and they are amazing. You can be reassuring, too, of course, but for someone who's depressed, this reaction feels incredibly invalidating, because that's not what their experience is. So, take a step back and let them do the talking. Listen to them first. Once they have emptied their bucket, once they have let all that negative energy out, it will be your turn to tell them you love them. Once they've poured all that toxicity out of their cup, they'll have more space for your love and reassurance.

Even though you don't want to monopolize the conversation or jump in to *fix the issue*, it is simultaneously important not to skirt it. Go ahead and ask your child the question that is on your mind:

Do you think that you could be depressed?

I often hear from parents that they are reluctant to ask this question; my clinical assessment is that this is because it can bring up a lot of guilt and shame for the parents. If your kid is depressed, that must mean that you are doing something wrong, right? If you were a better parent, then your child would be happier. Parents think that the better a job you do as a parent, the happier your child will be, the more successful they will be, the more engaged they will be.

But remember that clinical depression is not a reaction to something bad that has happened; that's what makes it "clinical." This direct question is often the one that cracks things open and makes way for them to accept help. Sometimes kids suspect that something is wrong, but they're afraid to admit it because it feels like weakness. If you raise this possibility, it is *helpful* and won't cause depression!

Remember that you need to build an alliance with your child— about their gaming behavior, and now also about their mood. They need to know that you two are on the same side of the issue. Encouraging your child to have a voice in the conversation is far more conducive to getting them to come around to the conclusion you've been hoping they come to all along—that they may have a problem with gaming (and possibly depression).

You don't want to drag them along *behind* you; you want to give them the freedom to walk their own path alongside you. Another great question that strengthens this alliance is "What do you think about getting evaluated by a therapist?"

Video Games and Anxiety

Anxiety is another issue many kids are struggling with these days, and, once again, its comorbidity with gaming is quite high. Anxiety is a little hard to define because it is basically an umbrella term that encompasses several discrete concepts. One is an emotion or a feeling: I feel anxious. Another is a cognitive process: I have anxious thoughts or I'm worried. While all people have anxious thoughts from time to time, when the thoughts, physiology, or emotions impair their ability to function, it rises to the level of an anxiety disorder.

Anxiety is basically a circuit in the brain that gets activated as we anticipate problems. It's also a protective mechanism: Once we can anticipate danger or problems, we can work to prevent them, thus protecting ourselves from future suffering. This is a survival instinct; humans are basically hardwired with anxiety.

From a yogic perspective, anxiety is the product of a future-focused mind. The yogis discovered that we are, by definition, anxious about things in the future. Even when we feel anxiety in the present, we are anticipating consequences in the future. Some people might feel they have "anxiety about the past"—but if you scratch the surface of that assumption, you realize that they are actually worrying about the future impact of past actions.

When our mind is focused on the present, the anxiety starts to feel better. This is exactly what video games ask your brain to do. This is also why treatments like meditation are so useful for anxiety, because meditation is simply training your mind to return to the present.

Anxiety is on the rise worldwide—we hear more and more about how mental health, generally, and anxiety, specifically, are getting worse. Why is that? Despite advances in medicine, despite more people being generally safer and more prosperous, why is anxiety increasing?

Some people think anxiety is on the rise due to societal and global changes—gender dynamics, climate insecurity, race relations, and so on. It makes sense that these big issues cause anxiety, but, from a medical perspective, there are two sources for anxiety: one is cognitive and one is physiological. Part of the reason we are having so much trouble managing anxiety these days is that, far too often, we are not addressing one of those two sources.

Cognitive anxiety is anxiety that is centered around particular fears or insecurities, learned behavior from particular experiences, often dating back to our childhood. On the other hand, physiological anxiety is how our bodies and brains literally create the experience of anxiety. When you're feeling anxious, there is all kinds of stuff going on in your body and in your brain. The adrenaline surge causes you to have sweaty palms; maybe your stomach feels a little bit nauseous.

When adrenaline travels to your brain, it also shapes your thought process. It causes hypotheticals to feel more real. It also reduces our cognitive flexibility, and we start seeing situations as black or white, rather than nuanced. Of course, when confronted by a tiger in the jungle, this kind of black-or-white thinking is a good thing. Our lives depend on fast action, on seeing the world as black and white in that moment.

Another stress hormone that's very important for anxiety is cortisol, which is a long-term stress hormone. When it gets activated by anxiety, it leads to other changes in our brain, including a change that prevents us from sleeping and relaxing. This is also beneficial in some circumstances—like in the jungle. After running away from a predator, our adrenaline shuts off. But cortisol is our long-term stress hormone, and it works for about twenty-four hours. After we've escaped from a tiger, we don't want to go into a deep sleep—we want a very light sleep, or even energy to keep us awake. (That tiger could still track us!)

The problem is that, in today's society, what triggers cortisol are things that staying awake at night won't help—like paying a mortgage, or being worried about a divorce, or your child's breakup. This is damaging because dealing with these kinds of things actually *require us to get a good night's sleep*, but our brain has evolved to keep us alive by keeping us awake.

Spiraling Thoughts

When we have an anxious thought, that thought tends to lead to other anxious thoughts, which, in turn, lead to other anxious thoughts, which, in turn, branch off to feed even more anxious thoughts. These thoughts quickly become overwhelming.

Unfortunately, however, no matter how much worrying you do about a problem, none of these spiraling thoughts actually fixes the problem. You are totally overwhelmed, but you haven't solved anything. These spiraling thought patterns, also known as "catastrophic" thinking, magnifying, or ruminating, are what make people with anxiety feel like they're trapped. People with anxiety tend to quell it by seeking reassurance from others, which, although it can alleviate our anxiety for a little while, also makes us dependent on the reassurance of others, sacrificing our freedom and independence. Of course, depending on others to provide reassurance—over and over and over again—can strain relationships, to say the least.

The other thing an anxious person will do to cope is seek out distractions. Video games are a great distraction. They basically force us to stop thinking the anxious thought—they help break the spiraling thought pattern. The problem is that once an anxious person discovers something that helps them cope with their anxiety, they will do it again and again. If your child suffers from anxiety, any time they feel anxious, they feel the need to game. This is a dangerous cycle, because, oftentimes, the amount of time your child spends gaming is one source of their anxiety.

I experienced this distraction loop myself. When I was falling further and further behind in Spanish, I knew that if I went to class, I'd be really embarrassed. I'd been missing class for a whole week. What would people think when I showed up? What would my professor say? My anxiety about returning to class led me to game more. Then a problem that had been mildly solvable at one week turned into two weeks—far more difficult. At three weeks, everything felt impossible. How would I ever go back to Spanish class again? Anxiety spike—cue more gaming. More gaming? Cue falling further behind in Spanish class. Which caused more anxiety, which led to even more gaming.

We also know from brain scans that the parts of our brain that experience anxiety are suppressed during gaming. The problem is that these measures are temporary; they do nothing to address the underlying issues. As soon as the game ends, the anxiety comes roaring back.

Also, remember that the more time your child spends online, the more their social skills atrophy. The worse their social skills get, the harder it is for them to socialize, thus increasing their isolation. The more isolated and anxious they feel, the more they end up gaming.

How can you help your child deal with anxiety in ways other than to disappear into a video game? You'll need to start with a conversation.

Talking about Anxiety

Communicating about anxiety is similar to communicating about depression. You want to ask open-ended questions:

> *Do you and your friends ever talk about anxiety? Is that something that affects you?*

> *Can you help me understand how that feels?*

> *How do you deal with it?*

As always, you will want to use a lot of reflective listening and empathic statements in the middle:

> *Wow, that sounds really tough. It sounds like anxiety gets in the way of a lot of things you might enjoy. In what ways does it get in the way of your life?*

Before you jump to a solution, you can ask:

> *Is that something that you'd want to work on actively? Would you want to have a conversation about trying to change things there?*

Keep the conversation that follows open-ended.

As with so much of parenting, this isn't a one-and-done conversation. Several conversations spaced out over time are far more effective at helping create long-lasting change. It's also important not to push your child into anything, because if you push, they will push back.

In these conversations, you don't want to set a boundary on the conversation. Instead, try to create a vacuum, a safe, available space where this conversation can occur, now or later. Once that vacuum is created, don't try to fill it; rather, take a step back and let the conversation unfurl over time, sometimes over days or weeks or even months. In time, your child will want to fill in the space you have created.

Once you've made some headway at getting on the same side of this topic, you will want to bring your child to a clinician for an evaluation. The question to ask is this:

What do you think about seeing someone to get an evaluation?

Don't jump to emphasizing treatment without first going through a proper evaluation. Start, as usual, with learning more.

CHAPTER 15

Challenge #4: Video Games and Marijuana Use

The popular wisdom is that addictive technology—video games—and addictive substances go hand in hand. This is for good reason: There is a very high comorbidity rate between the two—about 30 percent. In other words, if you are the parent of a gamer who is addicted to video games, there's about a 30 percent chance that they also use marijuana.

This is an increasingly problematic issue nowadays. When you were a kid, easy access to marijuana was far from a given. These days, marijuana is much more freely available, now that it has been decriminalized, if not commercialized, in many states and other countries. Vaping has skyrocketed among adolescents, not surprisingly—vape pens are easily accessible, as are an abundance of weed-related products, such as chocolates, gummies, mints, and tinctures. Even in states where marijuana is still criminalized, there are loopholes—mail-order options, online local pot purveyors, let alone access to alternative "legal" products like hemp-derived THC.

Gamers Are Extra-Vulnerable

There are a few reasons that gamers are especially vulnerable to marijuana usage. First and foremost, it's basic neurochemistry at play. A common experience of frequent gamers is that activities besides gaming don't seem fun, and even gaming itself can stop feeling fun after some time. In technical terms, this is called "dopaminergic tolerance."

To compensate for the lack of enjoyment, people will frequently use marijuana, which enhances the experience, as it does the experience of other entertainments—food, music, and sexual intercourse, for example (cannabinoids affect the *anandamide* receptor, which comes from the Sanskrit word for "bliss").

Beyond neurochemistry, behavioral science is involved, too. Since both video games and marijuana are often used to cope with difficult social or emotional issues, the combination of the two can sometimes create synergistic experiences, which makes things more fun. But pot can also make things more damaging. If marijuana helps you forget your problems, and gaming helps you forget your problems—wow, those two together really, *really* help you forget your problems. But the less you think about your problems, the harder they are to solve.

This spiral can get dangerous, and quite quickly. Kids who are socially anxious often turn to video games to forge a sense of community. Unfortunately, as kids play more and more online games, their social skills atrophy even further, which, of course, leads to worsening social anxiety.

As their level of social anxiety continues to increase, they start to use marijuana to help them socialize and feel more normal. This increasing dependence on marijuana to be able to socialize compounds the downward spiral. Socialization becomes even harder, which, in turn, causes them—you guessed it—to retreat into their online community even further. The cycle continues.

Beyond the neurochemical and behavioral risks, there are cultural ones, too. Unfortunately, marijuana culture often overlaps with gaming culture. Both cultures tend to bond around a general rejection of mainstream society. Like gamers, "potheads" are also sometimes ostracized by society—branded as good-for-nothings. In my years working with gamers, I've frequently seen young adults who, as they play more and more hours of video games and start to stall out in life, gravitate to the community of others who have also stalled.

As we all know, marijuana can be used medically or recreationally, and it's legal—even for eighteen-year-olds—in many states and countries. But we know that marijuana use is bad for developing brains. Period. Although some people are functional on pot, a lot of people aren't.

Scientists have yet to prove that marijuana use reduces IQ. Some studies show that its use reduces IQ by four to eight points; others show no change. But even if marijuana doesn't have a marked impact on IQ levels, it is still problematic because it negatively affects the parts of our brain that control motivation, and it affects how likely we are to follow through on goals. That does not mean that productive people don't use marijuana, but if you take a hundred people who use marijuana and a hundred people who don't, chances are that the hundred nonusers will be more productive and motivated than the users.

Another reason to worry: Marijuana is a gateway drug. If we use it in adolescence, it alters our dopamine circuitry, making us more vulnerable to other dopaminergic substances. In other words, marijuana use in the developing brain makes us more vulnerable to becoming addicted to other things.

Confronting Marijuana Use

Assessing your child's use of marijuana takes us back to the same methodology we have used all along—building an alliance, asking open-ended questions, and using reflective listening—to talk to your child about drugs. None of this means you are condoning its use, but talking about the issue as a way to start addressing it is very important.

If you have been with me all this time, but now you're drawing a line—*Drugs are completely off-limits, not just for us, but even for discussion*—please think about reconsidering. I have found these strategies incredibly effective for dealing with drug use by gamers; I ask you to at least consider trying my approach first.

The first step is, of course, understanding that this could be an issue for your child. Most parents aren't even aware of their child's marijuana use, since many children are not willing to disclose their substance use to their parents. Oftentimes, the parents who are *sure* that their kids don't use marijuana are the ones who are the least likely to notice the problem—because it isn't even a possibility in their mind that their child would ever do such a thing.

Second, understand that getting your child to stop smoking or ingesting marijuana may be difficult. Because just like with gaming, their usage isn't just about the marijuana itself. Your child might feel that marijuana is one of the few things that allows them to function normally in a social sense, and perhaps function normally emotionally, too.

The hardest patients I've had to work with are exactly those kids—ones for whom marijuana makes them feel normal. They see other kids their age living regular lives—socializing, having romantic interactions, living a relaxed, fun life as a teenager. But they can't relax. They can't sleep. They can't socialize. They feel awkward around the people they're attracted to. Enter marijuana, which allows them to enjoy themselves in all these types of situations. It suddenly allows them to live life "normally"—to have access to all the things that ordinary teenagers have.

As with gaming, the resistance you are going to encounter is based on their beliefs about what marijuana offers them. You will have to figure out how you can counterbalance those beliefs and fulfill those needs in a healthier way.

Start the Conversation

How should you approach the topic with them? You already know the answer—you're going to ask open-ended, judgment-free questions, and you're going to reflectively listen to their responses. Build an alliance on this subject, too—you want to build toward increasingly open communication on this issue.

Bring it up with them in a conversational, rather than a combative, manner. Leave any discussion of limits or punishment entirely off the table. Here are some examples of open-ended icebreakers:

I've heard that a lot of gamers use pot. It's something I'm curious about, and I want to know more about the two. Is it okay if we talk about it?

I've read that vape-pen use is skyrocketing. Can you tell me about vaping?

Do your friends use pot?

If you used pot, would you feel comfortable telling me?

How do you imagine I would react if you did use pot?

This conversation will get modified depending on the age of your child. If your child is older, they might be willing to be open to having a more thoughtful conversation with you on the topic. Once the topic of their own use has been broached, you can ask questions about how they think the drug affects them.

Do you think using marijuana affects your motivation in any way?

What has changed since you started using pot more?

Many older kids using pot are aware that although they enjoy the feeling the drug gives them, it does get in the way of them reaching some of their day-to-day goals. If you can talk about this, you might be able to get them on the same page about setting some limitations on their marijuana use.

Discussing Drug Use with Younger Adolescents

If you have a young teen—perhaps thirteen or fourteen—it might be extremely difficult to get them to open up about their marijuana use. But if you can start to chip away at such a big, intimidating topic by bringing it up generally—even if it's just related to references to pot in movies or music you might be watching or listening to together— you might be surprised at their willingness to share their experience. For example:

> *I hear a lot of references to weed in the music you and your friends listen to. Do any of you guys actually know someone who uses pot? What do people you know say about it?*

> *That movie made marijuana use seem sort of silly and fun. What have you heard about smoking weed?*

> *A lot of new marijuana dispensaries are popping up. I see them all the time when we drive to visit Grandma on the weekend. What do you think about marijuana?*

> *I saw you notice the guy who was smoking a joint on the corner on our way to breakfast earlier. What do you think about the push for legalization or decriminalization of marijuana now that you can see it and smell it so many public places?*

> *Everyone seems to know more about marijuana now than we did when we were growing up. It was sort of frowned*

upon in our generation for being dangerous, but things seem different now. What do you think about the safety of marijuana?

A word to the wise: Be very careful with your reaction to their responses. They might be dreading a very angry or combative reaction, and their imagined reaction may be closer to the truth than how you think you may respond. If they believe that, they believe that for a reason. They have been taught to expect particular things from you—our children often know us better than we think.

If your child is not willing to have that conversation with you, you can try going meta. Say, "Hey, I'm concerned that you may be using pot. I'd love to talk to you about it, but the conversation is so difficult, I don't even know where to start. Do you have any ideas how we might be able to talk about it without getting into fights or shutting down communication?"

If you are careful with your judgment and thoughtful with your commentary, your child might get lulled into thinking the topic isn't as taboo as they might have feared. A space to discuss the subject might gradually open up.

Discussing Marijuana Use When It's Legal

If marijuana is legal where you live and your child is at or older than the legal age, you still don't have to allow it in your house if you don't condone its use. Still, you'll be better off by starting a conversation with questions, not limitations. Boundary setting is for kids who are young; the way we approach the marijuana conversation for kids of legal age has to be much more open-ended.

Your general strategy should be similar to the strategy above, with some small tweaks:

1. Ask open-ended questions to understand your child's reason for using pot.
2. Lay a firm boundary that marijuana use in your house isn't acceptable.
3. Offer strong alternatives, with the goal of meeting the needs pot provides. Marijuana provides some benefits—such as helping the user to relax, ease their social anxiety, and feel normal. Target those goals with healthier alternatives, such as psychotherapy, to alleviate social anxiety or low self-esteem.
4. Stay open to changing your mind about marijuana if you can't get your child to stop using it altogether. This is not to say you're committing to changing your mind, but if you are the "You can never use pot ever" parent, what is likely to end up happening? Your firmness doesn't necessarily correlate with decreased use.

If you aren't willing to be open to changing your mind, why would your child be? What are you modeling for them? The whole point is that we need to prepare our child to make mature decisions—but *making mature decisions* can't happen unless we actually *let them make the decision.*

Setting Boundaries Together

Once you and your child have gotten more comfortable discussing marijuana use, it's time to set appropriate boundaries. Setting boundaries does not necessarily mean that you are condoning marijuana use—not at all. Instead, you are trying to work *with* your child to establish some boundaries around their marijuana use, and you are simultaneously helping them develop other interests or skill sets that the marijuana use has been compensating for.

As you set off on this task, remember that alliance building and alliance protecting are critical. Try to set boundaries together; otherwise you'll find yourself back where you were at the beginning of this book—on opposite teams, constantly fighting and frustrated. You will lose the trust you've carefully built up, and you'll be back on the other side of the wall from your child, unable to communicate.

Last—or perhaps far sooner in some cases—it's time to seek mental health treatment. Gaming addiction is a difficult road. It might be far too much to tackle a drug addiction on top of that without professional help. There also may well be mental illness (anxiety, a mood disorder, depression) driving both. A therapist can help you and your child sort out which concerns to tackle first, and which might be easier to tackle later on.

How to Move Kids Along the Stages of Change

The Pre-Contemplation Stage

► *Characterized by:*
  - Lack of awareness.
  - Frequently involves denial.
► *Common Pitfalls:*
  - You try to "convince" them that they have a problem.
  - You force them into compliance using leverage, which damages the relationship and has only temporary effects. When the leverage or oversight goes away, so does the positive behavior.
► *Correct Approach:*
  - Open-ended questions. Get them to *think* about the problem.

- Nonjudgmental approach. If you are on the attack, they will be on the defensive. Instead, work *together* to learn about and better understand their behavior.

The Contemplation Stage

▶ *Characterized by:*
  - Ambivalence, or internal conflict.
  - Child acknowledges there are advantages and disadvantages, but the disadvantages aren't strong enough to warrant sustained attempts at change.
  - Frequently looks like short-term attempts at change, without consistency. On a given day, it is worth changing; the next day, it's not worth changing. Looks like mixed signals or mixed behavior.
▶ *Common Pitfalls:*
  - You "pounce" on the disadvantages and push the child toward changing.
  - "See! I've been saying this all along. I'm so glad you *finally* understand."
  - You amplify their acknowledgment of disadvantages, instead of taking a neutral stance.
  - You use your *own* logic of advantages or disadvantages instead of focusing on *their* impression of advantages and disadvantages.
▶ *Correct Approach:*
  - Sit with the ambivalence and be ready to offer both sides of the equation. If they focus on problems,

you point out the advantages that *they believe*. If they focus on benefits, you point out the problems that *they believe*.

- Acknowledge the "stuckness" of the situation. "Yes, you like gaming, but it's also causing problems. Yes, it is causing problems, but isn't it fun?"
- Use reflective listening—just give them back what they give you. You can use *exaggerated* reflections to gently nudge them in the right direction.

The Preparation Stage

► *Characterized by:*
- Child acknowledges that it is time to change.
- Child realizes that changing will yield benefits for themselves—things that they want.

► *Common Pitfalls:*
- You become overjoyed by your child's readiness to change, so you jump to solutions.
- You formulate a plan for success because you know your kid so well.
- You don't involve your child in the planning process.

► *Correct Approach:*
- Offer a menu of options. As a parent, you can add things to the list, but let them choose.
- Let the child choose the type and intensity of change.
- They know what is most likely to succeed.

The Action Stage

► *Characterized by:*
  • Everyone agrees it is time to make changes.
  • Even though the motivation is there, and things are thought out, it doesn't mean you will be successful.

► *Common Pitfalls:*
  • Both you and your child fail to recognize that this will be a work in progress, and that multiple failures will likely be necessary to achieve lasting success.
  • You have a tendency to slip back into leading or problem solving for your child, taking away their independence and agency in the process.
  • You hold the child to earlier "promises" or statements, instead of rolling with resistance, or using the right technique for a given stage. For instance, on a given day, your child may go back to denying that there is a problem. Give them space and ask questions to get back to where you were.

► *Correct Approach:*
  • Regular check-ins.
  • Let them lead the movement toward change.
  • Adhere to boundaries that are agreed upon but use reflective listening and open-ended questions to address concerns.

Program Timeline

M any parents find it helpful to have a specific timeline, a plan that they can follow week to week. Toward that end, here is an eight-week road map that follows the program I offer at Healthy Gamer. Note: Weeks 1 and 2 are devoted to you, the parent, getting oriented to what's ahead by reading the first two parts of this book. It's not that I expect you to take two weeks to read 117 pages, but rather that it's important for you to sit with what you are reading and learning and let it really sink in. Then you'll be ready to act!

WEEK 1:

Read part one.

WEEK 2:

Read part two, at least through chapter 6.

WEEK 3:

Start working on the new conversational techniques you learned in part two.

- Practice open-ended questions and reflective listening, ideally with someone besides your child.
- Have your first conversation with your child.
  - o Explain that, in the past, you've done what you think is best. But you now realize that you are instituting limits on gaming without understanding their perspective. Apologize, if necessary. Explain that you'd like to learn more about their gaming over the next month—without making any changes to the limits that currently exist. You hope that by understanding their perspective better, you can set limits that are more aligned with what they want.
  - o Invite them to talk to you once a week.
  - o Start by asking a few broad, open-ended questions.

WEEKS 4–6:

More conversation, using open-ended questions, with the goal of learning about their values.

- Use suggested questions in chapter 6 as a guideline.
  - o Start with super high-level questions, such as, "What is gaming like for you?"

o Move on to questions about values and psychological needs.

- The goal of these weeks is to discover what
  your child cares about, so that you can use
  that as your guiding star when setting limits. You are going to develop boundaries to
  help them achieve *their goals*, not yours.
- Try to assess their psychological needs
  through gaming: challenge and achievement, identity, community, and safety.

o As your child opens up (we see this after two to
three weeks of conversations), start to ask harder
questions: "What are the downsides of gaming?"

- Read parts 3 and 4 during this time.

o If relevant, add questions about mental health
during weeks 5+.

WEEKS 7–8:

*Start to share your perspective and lay the foundation for boundary-
setting.*

- Ask for permission to share your thoughts.
- Lay out your concerns—not to convince them, but simply to
  state your point of view. Invite them to reflectively listen.
  ("What do you understand about what I'm worried about?")
- Try to find common ground for their values and yours—and
  couch the boundary setting as a plan of attack to achieve
  their goals, not just yours.

- Think about your own limitations (foundations of boundary setting)—and share your initial thoughts about potential boundaries and targets.

WEEKS 8+:

Move through the steps of "Developing a Boundary Plan," part one (see page 154) and part two (see page 173).

SELECTED BIBLIOGRAPHY

Introduction

Kuss, Daria J. "Internet Gaming Addiction: Current Perspectives." *Psychology Research and Behavior Management* 6 (2013): 125–37.

Tao, Ran, et al. "Proposed Diagnostic Criteria for Internet Addiction." *Addiction* 105, no. 3 (2010): 556–64.

Chapter 1

Everitt, Barry J., and Trevor W. Robbins. "Neural Systems of Reinforcement for Drug Addiction: From Actions to Habits to Compulsion." *Nature Neuroscience* 8, no. 11 (2005): 1481–89.

Goldstein, Rita Z., and Nora D. Volkow. "Drug Addiction and Its Underlying Neurobiological Basis: Neuroimaging Evidence for the Involvement of the Frontal Cortex." *The American Journal of Psychiatry* 159, no. 10 (2002): 1642–52.

Kalivas, Peter W., and Nora D. Volkow. "The Neural Basis of Addiction: A Pathology of Motivation and Choice." *The American Journal of Psychiatry* 162, no. 8 (2005): 1403–13.

Kühn, S., et al. "The Neural Basis of Video Gaming." *Translational Psychiatry* 1 (2011): e53.

Kuss, Daria J., and Mark D. Griffiths. "Internet and Gaming Addiction: A Systematic Literature Review of Neuroimaging Studies." *Brain Sciences* 2, no. 3 (2012): 347–74.

Lingford-Hughes, Anne, and David Nutt. "Neurobiology of Addiction and Implications for Treatment." *The British Journal of Psychiatry* 182 (2003): 97–100.

Volkow, Nora D., Joanna S. Fowler, and Gene-Jack Wang. "The Addicted Human Brain: Insights from Imaging Studies." *The Journal of Clinical Investigation* 111, no. 10 (2003): 1444–51.

Yee, Nick. "The Labor of Fun: How Video Games Blur the Boundaries of Work and Play." *Games and Culture* 1, no. 1 (2006): 68–71.

Chapter 2

Bekir, Seyhan, and Eyup Celik. "Examining the Factors Contributing to Adolescents' Online Game Addiction." *Anales de Psicologia* 35, no. 3 (2019): 444–52.

Chang, Eunbi, and Boyoung Kim. "School and Individual Factors on Game Addiction: A Multilevel Analysis." *International Journal of Psychology* 55, no. 1 (2019): 822–31.

Maden, Cagtay, and Kezban Bayramlar. "Effects of Sedentary Lifestyle and Physical Activity in Gaming Disorder." *International*

Journal of Academic Medicine and Pharmacy 4, no. 2 (2022): 68–71.

Wei, Han-Ting, et al. "The Association Between Online Gaming, Social Phobia, and Depression: An Internet Survey." *BMC Psychiatry* 12 (2012): 92.

Chapter 4

Burke, Jeffrey. D., et al. "Developmental Transitions among Affective and Behavioral Disorders in Adolescent Boys." *Journal of Child Psychology and Psychiatry, and Allied Disciplines*, 46, no. 11(2005): 1200–10.

Connors, Gerald J., et al. *Substance Abuse Treatment and the Stages of Change: Selecting and Planning Interventions,* 2nd ed. New York: Guilford Press, 2013.

DiClemente, Carlo C., Debra Schlundt, and Leigh Gemmell. "Readiness and Stages of Change in Addiction Treatment." *The American Journal on Addictions* 13, no. 2 (2004): 103–19.

Johnston, Oliver G., et al. "Preliminary Validation of the Parental Help-Seeking Stage of Change Measure for Child Behavior Problems." *Child & Youth Care Forum* 49, no. 2 (2020): 223–46.

Krebs, Paul, et al. "Stages of Change." In *Psychotherapy Relationships that Work: Evidence-Based Therapist Responsiveness,* 3rd edition, edited by John C. Norcross and Bruce E. Wampold, 296–328. New York: Oxford Academic, 2019.

Maremmani, Angelo Giovanni Icro, et al. "Correlations Between Awareness of Illness (Insight) and History of Addiction in Heroin-Addicted Patients." *Frontiers in Psychiatry* 3 (2012): 61.

Chapter 5

Benítez, José L., et al. "Building an Expanded Therapeutic Alliance: A Task Analysis with Families Trapped in Parental-Adolescent Conflict." *Family Process* 59, no. 2 (2020): 409–27.

Bonnaire, Céline, Alexandre Har, and Howard Liddle. "Searching for Change Mechanisms in Emotion-Focused Work with Adolescents and Parents: An Example from Multidimensional Family Therapy." *Couple and Family Psychology: Research and Practice* 9, no. 2 (2020): 100–21.

Diamond, Gary M., et al. "Alliance-Building Interventions with Adolescents in Family Therapy: A Process Study." *Psychotherapy: Theory, Research, Practice, Training* 36, no. 4 (1999): 355.

Gilson, Maria Lisa, and Angela Abela. "The Therapeutic Alliance with Parents and Their Children Working through a Relational Trauma in the Family." *Contemporary Family Therapy* 43, no. 4 (2021): 343–58.

Chapter 7

Muñoz-Silva, Alicia, Rocio Lago-Urbano, and Manuel Sanchez-Garcia. "Family Impact and Parenting Styles in Families of Children with ADHD." *Journal of Child and Family Studies* 26, no. 3 (2017): 1–14.

Schiltz, Hillary K., et al. "Examining Differences in Parenting Stress, Parenting Efficacy, and Household Context among Mothers of Youth with Autism and/or ADHD." *Journal of Child and Family Studies* 31, no. 4 (2022): 774–89.

Stevens, Anne E., et al. "Maternal Parenting Style and Internalizing and ADHD Symptoms in College Students." *Journal of Child and Family Studies* 28, no. 1 (2019): 260–72.

Chapter 10

Beckwith, Vickie Z., and Jennifer Beckwith. "Motivational Interviewing: A Communication Tool to Promote Positive Behavior Change and Optimal Health Outcomes." *NASN School Nurse* 35, no. 6 (2020): 344–51.

Burke, Jeffrey D., Irwin Waldman, and Benjamin B. Lahey. "Predictive Validity of Childhood Oppositional Defiant Disorder and Conduct Disorder: Implications for the DSM-V." *Journal of Abnormal Psychology*, 119, no. 4 (2010): 739–51.

Chapter 11

Ferguson, Christopher J., Mark Coulson, and Jane Barnett. "A Meta-Analysis of Pathological Gaming Prevalence and Comorbidity with Mental Health, Academic and Social Problems." *Journal of Psychiatric Research* 45, no. 12 (2011): 1573–78.

Piao, Mei Ying, Eui Jun Jeong, and Jeong Ae Kim. "Mental Health of Parents and Their Children: A Longitudinal Study of the Effects of Parents' Negative Affect on Adolescents' Pathological Gaming." *Healthcare* 10, no. 11 (2022): 2233.

Pinquart, Martin, and Dana-Christina Gerke. "Associations of Parenting Styles with Self-Esteem in Children and Adolescents: A Meta-Analysis." *Journal of Child and Family Studies* 28, no. 2 (2019): 2017–35.

Tripathi, Shraddha, and Priyansha Singh Jadon. "Effect of Authoritarian Parenting Style on Self Esteem of the Child: A Systematic Review." *International Journal of Advance Research and Innovative Ideas in Education* 3 (2017): 909–13.

Yildiz Durak, Hatice, Abdulkadir Haktanir, and Mustafa Saritepeci. "Examining the Predictors of Video Game Addiction According to Expertise Levels of the Players: The Role of Time Spent on Video Gaming, Engagement, Positive Gaming Perception, Social Support and Relational Health Indices." *International Journal of Mental Health and Addiction* (2023): 1–26.

Chapter 13

Craig, Francesco, et al. "A Systematic Review of Problematic Video-Game Use in People with Autism Spectrum Disorders." *Research in Autism Spectrum Disorders* 82 (2021): 101726.

Kervin, Ryan, et al. "Behavioral Addiction and Autism Spectrum Disorder: A Systematic Review." *Research in Developmental Disabilities* 117 (2021): 104033.

ACKNOWLEDGMENTS

Om Sri Gurubhyo Namah. Salutations to all the teachers.

I'd like to start by thanking my parents, Uma and Dhadha, as well as Meenaxi and Pradip, without whom I would not be here today. A special thanks to Akash and Saurabh, who stepped in to help parent my children while I was on call at the hospital, speaking at conferences, or literally writing this book.

A huge thank you to the Kanojia, Gandhy, and Parekh clans, who have taught me not only how to be a good parent, but a good human. I'm especially grateful to Ba, whose blessings helped me become a doctor in the first place.

I'd also like to thank my gurus in India, who guided me away from the material world, then back toward life afterward. I'd like to thank Dr. Nagendra and the folks at Prashanti, for introducing me to yoga and meditation, as well as my teachers at the Bihar School of Yoga. Last, I'd like to thank my Guruji for mantra and kundalini diksha, which are the gifts that I owe most of my worldly success to.

On the medical side, my gratitude begins with Laura Snydman, who taught me to love medicine and encouraged me to follow my own path. I'd like to thank Jodi Schindelheim, who taught me to love psychiatry by eating an apple core. I'm also eternally grateful to Paul Summergrad for guiding my journey to becoming a doctor, becoming a psychiatrist, and even taking my first steps outside of clinical medicine.

I'm grateful to all of my attendings, supervisors, coresidents, and medical staff for helping me become a good doctor. A huge thanks to Felicia Smith and Scott Beach, for being kind enough to accept me into the best residency program in the world (for me, anyway). It is hard to find a place where one can learn to be an excellent doctor and to think beyond an individual patient. I'm especially grateful and still enamored with Ted Stern, Nick Kontos, John Querques, and John Taylor for creating a model for me to aspire to when I think "psychiatrist."

I'm also grateful to John Denninger for stepping in as a supervisor and guiding me when others didn't know how. Your support has been invaluable in helping me grow into the person I am today. I'd also like to thank Darshan Mehta for his long-term mentorship and helping me fall in love with the science of complementary and alternative medicine. I'm also grateful to Greg Fricchione for teaching me how to build something from the ground up.

I'd like to thank Jerry Rosenbaum for his guidance in how to think big but never forget the little people. I'm grateful to Scott Rauch for seeing where my talents truly lay and introducing me to the Institute of Coaching, which has been a second home of sorts. I'm grateful to Rocco Ianucci, Hilary Connery, Jen, and Kenny, who taught me how to see and help people who struggle with addictions.

In particular, I'm grateful to Tom McCoy for helping me not get canceled before I got started. I'd like to thank Liz Liebson for seeing me for who I am and charging me to "use my power for good, instead of evil"—I took your advice to heart and here we are!

A huge shout out to my coresidents and partners in crime who made what is regarded by most as a grueling experience into something I loved and even miss. A special thanks for Daniel Daunis, Judy Puckett, Nicole Benson, and Gowri Aragam.

Next, I'd like to thank my patients, who have taught me more about medicine and allowed me to help more people than all of the doctors, mentors, and supervisors put together. The tools in this book were granted to me by you.

I'm also grateful to the Heathy Gamer Community, that nebulous, amorphous mass of chatters from the internet, who are the only people who could have taught me more than my patients. Chat told me to write a book, and here it is. I know it isn't what you guys expected, but we gotta help the next crew of little chatters and their parents. I promise you've got dibs on the next book. A special shout out to the WVG discord, who are truly healthy gamers, tolerating my rusty skills. In the rest of the world, I may be a somebody, but with y'all, I'm the runt of the litter.

And this book could not be written without all the amazing staff at the HG company, as well as my agents Byrd Leavell and Dan Milaschewski. A huge thank you to Marnie Cochran and Jane Fleming Fransson for their patience in working with me (I promise I'll do better if we get a next time) and who turned what was a steaming pile of academic indecipherableness into a legible book that may actually help a human being.

Acknowledgments

To save the best for last, thank you to my lovely wife, Kruti, for seven lifetimes of marriage that feel like a joy. Looking forward to the next six. And lastly, to my favorite humans on the planet, Vera and Avi, for being nothing more or nothing less than what you are. I love you.

INDEX

ABOUT THE AUTHOR

Dr. Alok Kanojia, also known as "Dr. K," is a Harvard-trained psychiatrist specializing in mental health for the gaming community. He is the president and cofounder of Healthy Gamer, a mental health platform that provides content, coaching, and community resources to help young people take control of their mental health and their lives. A highly sought-after speaker and media expert, he and his wife live in Houston, Texas, with their two young daughters.

www.healthygamer.gg